Ready for

PET

With Answer Key

Nick Kenny Anne Kelly

A complete course for the Preliminary English Test

Macmillan Education
Between Towns Road, Oxford OX4 3PP
A division of Macmillan Publishers Limited
Companies and representatives throughout the world

ISBN   1 405 01407 5 (without Key)
        1 405 01406 7 (with Key)

Text © Nick Kenny and Anne Kelly
Design and illustration © Macmillan Publishers Limited 2003

First published 2001
This edition 2003

Designed by Jim Evoy
Illustrated by Mike Atkinson; David Smith; Martin Saunders;
Peter Harper; Ken Harvey
Cover design by Andrew Oliver

The authors would like to thank Barbara Lewis, David Foll,
Penny Beck and Margaret van Doelen for their help with
this book.

The publishers would like to thank the following
consultants and teachers for piloting and reviewing this
book: Andy Hannaford, Anthony Matthews, Barbara Lewis,
Gail Butler, Mabel Turner and Sarah Ellis.

The authors and publishers would like to thank the
following for permission to reproduce copyright material:
University of Cambridge Local Examinations Syndicate for
the answer sheets on pp.92–3.
Adapted extracts from 'Living in the past' by Jerome
Monahan, The Guardian Education, 18 July 2000. Copyright
© Jerome Monahan, and reproduced with his permission;
Adapted extracts from 'We crossed a land of ice' by Suzanne
Stevenson, Metro, 25 September 2001. Reproduced by
permission of Metro; Adapted extracts from 'It's a whale of
a time' by Sarah Tucker, Travel Metro, 21 November 2001.
Reproduced by permission of Metro; Adapted extracts from
'Idol Pleasures' by Sara O'Reilly, Time Out London, 26 June–3
July 2002. Copyright © Time Out Group, and reproduced by
kind permission of Time Out Group.

The authors and publishers would like to thank the
following for permission to reproduce their photographs:
Alamy p31(m); Sue Baker © MELT p18(br); Corbis / Michael
Dunn pp25(tr), Corbis / David Giles 25(tl), Corbis / Stephanie
Colasanti 51, Corbis / Wartenberg 60, Corbis RF, 78 (r,l),
91(b); Haddon Davies © MELT pp16 (2,3), 54(5); English
Heritage Photo Library p31(t,b); Eye Ubiquitous / Craig
Hutchins pp39, 41(b), 48(ml), Eye Ubiquitous / Tim Hawkins
48(m), Eye Ubiquitous / Julia Waterlow 48(mr); Chris
Honeywell © MELT p18(tr); Image Bank pp43, 63(t); MELT
pp16 (1,4,5), 28, 54 (1,2,3,4), 56 (all); Photodisk p47(t), Pictor
p63(b); Stone pp19, 33, 41(t), 42, 47(b), 91(t); Sunday Times
(Funday Times) p44; Taxi pp6, 12(tr),27, 38 ; John Walmsley
p12(tl).

Cover and title page photos
©Thinkstock (ml), ©Digital Vision (l, mr), ©Photodisk (r)

Printed and bound in Thailand

2007   2006   2005
10 9 8 7 6 5 4 3

With Answer Key

10 9 8 7 6 5 4

Contents

Introduction

Ready for PET is for students of English who are preparing to take the University of Cambridge Preliminary English Test (PET). *Ready for PET* will get you ready for this test in three important ways. First, it will give you practice in doing the kinds of exercises you will do in the test. Then, it will give you advice on how you can do your best in these exercises. Finally, it will help you learn the vocabulary you need to do the writing and speaking exercises fluently. In this way, you can feel confident about your English when you do the test.

You can use *Ready for PET* in your English class with your teacher, or you can use it to get ready for the test by yourself.

What is the Preliminary English Test (PET)?

The University of Cambridge has tests for students of English at five different levels, from beginners to very advanced students.

PET is at level 2 and is for lower intermediate students. PET tests your reading, writing, listening and speaking. You get 25% of the total marks for the test for each of these four skills. There are three different papers.

Paper 1 is Reading and Writing and takes 1 hour and 30 minutes. In this paper, there are five reading parts and three writing parts. In the reading part of the paper, you have to read some texts and answer some questions on each one. For these questions, you answer by choosing A, B, C, or D. In the writing part of the paper, you have to do a short grammar exercise, write a short message, and then write a letter or story. This is a summary of the Reading and Writing paper:

Paper 1: Reading and Writing (1 hour 30 minutes)			
	Type of text	Type of question	Number of questions and marks
Reading			
Part 1	five signs, notices or messages	reading comprehension: multiple choice	5
Part 2	eight short texts	reading comprehension: matching	5
Part 3	one text	reading comprehension: correct/not correct	10
Part 4	one text	reading comprehension: multiple choice	5
Part 5	one text	vocabulary and grammar: multiple choice	10
Writing			
Part 1		grammar	5
Part 2		writing a short message	1 question: 5 marks
Part 3		writing a letter or story	1 question: 15 marks

Paper 2 is Listening and takes about 30 minutes. There are four parts to the paper. You have to listen to a recording and answer some questions. For the questions for three parts, you answer by choosing A, B, or C and for one part you write down a few words or numbers. You hear each part of the recording twice. This is a summary of the Listening paper:

	Type of text	Type of question	Number of questions and marks
	Paper 2: Listening (approximately 30 minutes)		
Part 1	seven short recordings (one or two people speaking)	multiple choice pictures	7
Part 2	one or two people speaking	multiple choice	6
Part 3	one person speaking	writing down words	6
Part 4	two people speaking	correct/not correct	6

Paper 3 is Speaking and takes 10–12 minutes. There are four parts to the paper. You do the Speaking test with another student. In the Speaking test, you and your partner talk to an examiner and to each other, while another examiner listens to you. The examiner will ask you some questions and give you some instructions about what you should talk about. In two parts, you have some pictures to talk about. This is a summary of the Speaking paper:

	Paper 3: Speaking (10–12 minutes)
Part 1	The examiner asks you and your partner questions about yourselves.
Part 2	You and your partner look at some pictures showing a situation and talk about it together.
Part 3	You and your partner take it in turns to describe a photograph each.
Part 4	You and your partner have a conversation about the subject (eg holidays) of your photos.

You will find more detailed information about each part of all three papers in the different lessons of *Ready for PET*.

How *Ready for PET* is organized

There are ten units in *Ready for PET* and each unit has two lessons. In each unit, you will find exercises to practise the reading, writing, listening and speaking skills, and the vocabulary and grammar you will need in PET. In each lesson of Units 1–8 there is detailed information and advice about one particular part of the test, and in Units 9–10 you can revise all the advice that has gone before. Throughout the book there are **Get ready** boxes containing clear, helpful exam tips.

At the end of the book there are two PET practice tests. When you do these, you will experience what it is like taking the real test. You will see how much time you have to do each question and you will find out which parts of the test you need to practise more.

When you've worked through *Ready for PET*, you'll know what to expect in every part of the test, and you'll have the language you need to do the test well.

For students studying alone

If you are preparing for PET without a teacher, *Ready for PET* will help you. You should use *Ready for PET* at the same time as your general English coursebook. Your coursebook will develop your knowledge of English, and *Ready for PET* will give you the special practice you need for the test exercises.

Remember to use the 'with key' edition of *Ready for PET,* which has a key to exercises and tapescripts of the listening texts at the back. When you have finished each exercise, check your answers with the key. Don't look at the key until you have done each exercise. If necessary, you can use a dictionary to help you with unknown words, but always try to guess the meaning of words first. You should also see if you can answer the questions without knowing the difficult words.

The texts of the listening exercises are on cassette (or CD). In the PET Listening test, you hear each listening text twice, so when you are practising with these exercises, rewind the tape and listen again before checking your answers. If you don't understand something you can look at the tapescript, but never do this until you have listened to the tape twice.

There are many writing exercises in *Ready for PET*. It's useful if you can ask a teacher to correct these for you, but it doesn't matter if this isn't possible. Just doing the writing is good practice. Always make sure you follow the instructions exactly and check your own work carefully.

There are also many speaking exercises in the book. It's difficult to do speaking exercises if you're studying alone, but it's important that you get speaking practice. Remember, 25% of the marks for the whole of PET are for the Speaking test, so if possible, do the speaking exercises with another student. If you can't do this, do the exercises by yourself, speaking into a cassette recorder. Then listen to yourself speaking and think of ways in which you could do the exercise better. Don't worry about making mistakes, but try to express your ideas clearly.

On pages 66–91, there are two practice tests. You should try to do at least one of these like a real test. Only take the amount of time allowed for the test, and do it without any dictionary or notes to help you.

Before you start, decide how many hours a week you can spend studying with *Ready for PET* and keep to this decision. It is better to study regularly for short periods than to try and do everything just before the day of the test.

The PET preparation diary on the opposite page will help you to organize your study. Fill in the date you start your PET preparation at the top, and the date you will take PET at the bottom. Then work out how many days or weeks you have to complete each unit of this book. When you have completed a unit, write the date in the space provided, and decide how well you have done in the different practice exercises in that unit (self-assessment). In the 'Study notes' section you can write anything which will help you. For example, you may want to make a note of some exercises you want to look at again, or some exercises which you haven't had time to do and plan to work on later. You should organize your study in the way which best suits you in the time you have available before you take PET.

PET preparation diary

I began preparing for PET on: (date) ....

Unit	Study notes	Self-assessment ✔ = I did well ✗ = I need more practice
1 completed on		Reading Listening Speaking Writing Vocabulary
2 completed on		Reading Listening Speaking Writing Vocabulary
3 completed on		Reading Listening Speaking Writing Vocabulary
4 completed on		Reading Listening Speaking Writing Vocabulary
5 completed on		Reading Listening Speaking Writing Vocabulary
6 completed on		Reading Listening Speaking Writing Vocabulary
7 completed on		Reading Listening Speaking Writing Vocabulary
8 completed on		Reading Listening Speaking Writing Vocabulary
9 completed on		Reading Speaking Writing Vocabulary
10 completed on		Reading Listening Speaking Writing Vocabulary

I am taking PET on: (test date) ....

Personal information

1 **Writing**

Complete this form with information about yourself.

PERSONAL FACTFILE
Name: ....
Surname: ....
Address: ....
....
Sex: ....
Age: ....
Occupation: ....
Interests: ....
....
....
....

2 **Listening** 😀

1 Listen to two people talking about themselves and complete their personal factfiles.

PERSONAL FACTFILE

Name: ....
Surname: ....
Address: ....
....
Sex: ....
Age: ....
Occupation: ....
Interests: ....
....
....
....

A

PERSONAL FACTFILE

Name: ....
Surname: ....
Address: ....
....
Sex: ....
Age: ....
Occupation: ....
Interests: ....
....
....
....

B

2 If you wanted to find out more information about these people, what questions would you ask? Make questions beginning with each of these words.

Are... ?

When... ?

What... ?

Do... ?

Where... ?

How... ?

3 Speaking

1 **Look at the activities in the box. Which of these activities are you good at? Order the activities from most interesting (1) to least interesting (12).**

Talk about why you like (1) and why you dislike (12).

watching sports	playing sports	computer games
watersports	collecting things	playing a musical instrument
dancing	learning languages	making things
driving	keep-fit exercises	surfing the Internet

2 **How do you spell your name? Practise saying the letters in English.**

3 **Listen to five people spelling their names. Write their names below:**

1 .... 2 .... 3 ....
4 .... 5 ....

Get ready for PET Speaking Part 1

1 In Part 1 of the PET Speaking test, the examiner will ask you questions about yourself. For example, there will be questions about:
- your home and family
- what you do every day
- your work or studies
- things you enjoy or don't enjoy doing

2 When you answer the questions, say what you really think and explain why. Answer the questions directly; don't talk about yourself in general.

3 Make the conversation interesting by adding extra information. Don't just give short answers.

4 During Part 1, the examiner will ask you to spell your name. Practise spelling both your first name and your surname. Make sure you can do this perfectly.

5 Remember, in Part 1 you talk to the examiner, not to your partner.

4 Writing

Complete the second sentence so that it means the same as the first, using no more than three words.

1 Do you play football well?
Are you a .... player?

2 Do watersports interest you?
Are you .... watersports?

3 What is your age?
How .... you?

4 Which is your favourite school subject?
Which school subject .... like best?

5 How is your surname spelt?
How do .... your surname?

5 Writing

You have decided to join an English-language club on the Internet. Write a brief description of yourself for the database. You can write up to 100 words. Remember to include:

- your personal details, for example, name and age
- what you do/study
- the things that you are interested in

6 Listening 🔊

1 David and Victoria have just met at a party. Complete the gaps in their conversation using the phrases below. Write the correct letters in the spaces.

David: Hello. I'm David.

Victoria: **(1)** ....

David: Yes, I'm one of his friends too, and we play football together. What do you study?

Victoria: **(2)** ....

David: I've finished college, actually, and I'm working as a windsurfing instructor.

Victoria: **(3)** ....

David: That doesn't matter. You could learn.

Victoria: **(4)** ....

David: So am I. I'm running a course which starts next week. Would you be interested in joining?

Victoria: **(5)** ....

Use five of these phrases to complete Victoria's part of the conversation.

A English. Have you finished college?

B Yes, I suppose so. But what I'm really interested in is sailing.

C Hi. I'm Victoria. I'm a friend of Tom's from college.

D Hello, I'm Victoria. I'm really interested in football.

E I'm doing languages. What about you?

F Oh, I'm really interested in watersports, but I'm not very good at windsurfing.

G Oh... I might be... it depends.

🔊 **2 Which two didn't you use? Now listen and check.**

3 When you meet someone of your own age for the first time:

* what questions do you ask them?
* what are good things to talk about?
* what do you tell them about yourself?

7 Reading

1 Look at these notices and choose the correct explanation, A, B, or C.

This notice is telling you   **1**

A what information to write.

B which type of letters to use.

C which type of pen to use.

> Please write in
> BLOCK CAPITALS

This notice is giving you   **2**

A some advice.

B a suggestion.

C an instruction.

> **ALL PACKAGES
> MUST BE
> SIGNED FOR**

2 What is a signature? How is it different from other ways of writing your name?

Write your name in block capitals: ....

Write your signature: ....

1 Vocabulary

1 Match the words in A with the words in B. For example, *comb* **and** *hair* **go together. Some words are used more than once.**

A

attend	boil	brush	clean	comb
dial	dust	feed	iron	miss
tidy	tie	wash		

B

bus	class	desk	dishes
furniture	hair	meeting	number
pet	shirt	shoes	
shoelaces	teeth	water	

Which of these things do you do regularly, sometimes, occasionally, or never? Talk about some of your habits using the words in the boxes.

2 Now match the words in C with the words in D. Some words are used more than once.

C

hand in	join in	take off
put on	put up	put away
turn up	plug in	turn on

D

books	game	homework
make-up	music	radio
socks	umbrella	light

Use the words in the boxes to talk about your daily life.

2 Reading

What kinds of short message do you write to people in your daily life? Read these short messages.

A

Mum,
All my white sports shirts are dirty! I must wear a clean one in the tennis match tomorrow. Could you wash and iron one for me? If you can, I'll wash up after dinner every night for a week! Thanks a lot.
Julia

B

E-mail:

To: Paulo
From: Emilio

Thanks for telling me about the English homework. I'm worried I won't be able to do it because I missed the lesson. Why don't you come to my house on Saturday and we can do the exercises together?

C

POSTCA

Dear Gemma,
My cousin Lou and I visited Brighton yesterday. What a pity you couldn't come with us! We went shopping, and then we visited a beautiful old palace called Brighton Pavilion. My favourite part of the day was eating ice-cream on the beach.
Love, Jodie

In which message (or messages), is the writer

1 thanking someone for something?
2 describing what he/she has done?
3 explaining why he/she needs to have something?
4 telling someone what he/she liked best about something?
5 asking someone to do something for him/her?
6 saying how he/she feels about something?
7 suggesting an activity?
8 offering to do something?

3 Writing

1 Imagine this situation and then write a short message to a classmate.
You want to ask a classmate to help you do something.
Write a note to your classmate. In your note, you should

- explain what help you'd like your classmate to give you
- suggest a time when your classmate can help you
- offer to do something for your classmate

Write 35–45 words.

2 Read your classmate's note to you and then write another note in reply.
In your note, you should

- agree to help your classmate
- suggest a *different* time to give this help
- accept your classmate's offer

Write 35–45 words.

Get ready for PET Writing Part 2

1 The first line of the instructions describes a situation to you. Read this carefully and imagine the situation.
2 The instructions tell you to write *three* points in your message. Make sure you say something about each point.
3 Remember to address your message to the person named in the instructions (eg *Dear Alice, Hi Ben*).
4 Don't forget to write your name at the end of your message.
5 Don't write fewer than 35 words or more than 45 words.
6 Check what you have written.

3 Write one of these short messages.
Your English friend, Alice, helped you with your English homework last week.
Write a card to send to Alice. In your card, you should

- thank Alice
- tell her what your teacher said about your homework
- suggest when you could see Alice again

Write 35–45 words.

You took a phone call for your English friend, Ben, about a parcel.
Write the phone message for Ben. In your message, you should

- tell Ben who phoned
- say what is in the parcel
- explain what Ben should do when the parcel arrives

Write 35–45 words.

4 Writing

There are several ways to make comparisons.
Examples:

*Sam listens to the radio **more** often **than** Marcia does.*
*Marcia listens to the radio **less** often **than** Sam does.*
*Marcia doesn't listen to the radio **as** often **as** Sam does.*

*My shoes are clean**er than** my brother's.*
*My brother's shoes are dirt**ier than** mine.*
*My brother's shoes aren't **as** clean **as** mine.*

*My grandmother is **better** at ironing **than** my mother.*
*My mother is not **as** good at ironing **as** my grandmother.*
*My mother is **worse** at ironing **than** my grandmother.*

Complete the second sentence so that it means the same as the first, using no more than three words.

1 Your bedroom is tidier than mine.
   My bedroom isn't .... yours.

2 Gerry doesn't do the washing-up as fast as Paul.
   Paul does the washing-up .... Gerry.

3 The new armchair isn't nearly as comfortable as the old one.
   The old armchair is much .... the new one.

4 Every evening, Sally does a lot more homework than Rachel.
   Every evening, Rachel does a lot .... Sally.

5 This music isn't nearly as bad as the music they play on Radio 2.
   The music they play on Radio 2 is far .... this music.

5 Reading

1 **What inventions of the last 2,000 years have caused the most important changes in people's daily lives?**

2 **Read this text and choose the correct word, A, B, C or D for each space.**

INVENTIONS OF THE LAST 2,000 YEARS

Recently, hundreds of scientists and philosophers were asked to name the most important invention of the last 2,000 years. You might **(1)** .... people to say the Internet, penicillin or the internal combustion engine, but in **(2)** .... nobody did. One scientist **(3)** .... for paper because, long before the Internet, paper allowed ideas to be sent around the world. **(4)** .... scientists agreed that modern medicine has helped millions of people, but said **(5)** .... inventions, such as soap and pipes for clean and dirty water, have **(6)** .... more lives. One philosopher said hay was the most important because it's winter food for horses. Without **(7)** .... , horses couldn't exist in cold climates, **(8)** .... meant that there couldn't be cities in places colder than Athens and Rome. So, thanks **(9)** .... hay, Vienna, Paris, London and Berlin were built! Someone else named the mirror because in **(10)** .... at our own faces we can learn about human beings in general.

1	**A** expect	**B** think	**C** believe	**D** guess
2	**A** all	**B** fact	**C** particular	**D** detail
3	**A** suggested	**B** judged	**C** answered	**D** voted
4	**A** Other	**B** Another	**C** Others	**D** Any
5	**A** clearer	**B** plainer	**C** simpler	**D** purer
6	**A** rescued	**B** delivered	**C** saved	**D** recovered
7	**A** them	**B** it	**C** these	**D** many
8	**A** what	**B** that	**C** where	**D** which
9	**A** to	**B** of	**C** by	**D** from
10	**A** seeing	**B** looking	**C** watching	**D** studying

You live and learn

1 | **Vocabulary** **1** Look at the photographs.

A

B

In which of the photos can you see these things?

mouse	screen	desk
blackboard	keyboard	pen
chair	map	

somebody...	asking	thinking
	talking	reading
	explaining	waiting

2 What other things can you see in the photographs?

2 | **Speaking** **1** Look at these ideas. Which five do you think are the best ways to learn English?

surfing the Internet   listening to songs
studying a textbook   watching satellite TV
going to classes   **?**   talking to people in English
playing computer games   watching films in English
doing grammar exercises   reading newspapers and magazines

2 Listen to Polly. She is studying Spanish.

- Which is her favourite way of studying Spanish?
- Choose the correct picture.

A ☐

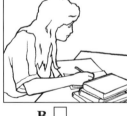
B ☐

C ☐

- Why does Polly like studying in this way?

3 You want to ask Polly about the things in the box below. Write the questions.

the teacher	length of each class	number of students
the book(s) and equipment	type of people	cost of course
the classroom	number of classes per week	what she's learnt

3 Speaking

1 **Look at this situation.**

A young friend of yours wants to learn a new language in his free time.
He has a small amount of money to spend on this new hobby.
First talk about the things he can buy to help him learn the language.
Then say which will be the best use of his money.

Look at these ways of starting the discussion.
Where shall we begin?
Let's talk about x first.
How about ..., what do you think of that idea?

Look at these ways of saying what you think.
I think ... is a good idea because...
I think ... is better than ... because...
I think (s)he should buy ... because....
I think the best thing (for him/her) to buy is ... because...

Look at these ways of responding to what your partner says.
That's a good idea because...
I'm not so sure about that because...
And what do you think about ...?

Get ready for PET Speaking Part 2

1 Listen to the instructions. Are you talking about yourself or somebody else?

2 Speak to your partner, not to the examiner.

3 Remember to *listen* to your partner and *respond* to what (s)he says.

4 Say *what* you think and explain *why* you think it.

2 **Pietro and Valerie are doing exercise 3.1. Complete the gaps in their conversation using the phrases below. Write the correct letters in the spaces.**

Valerie: So, our friend wants to learn a new language?
Pietro: **(1)** ....
Valerie: No, he can't. Let's start by talking about which of them will be useful for him.
Pietro: **(2)** ....
Valerie: OK. Shall we start with this one, the dictionary?
Pietro: **(3)** ....
Valerie: Yes, I agree, and it's also good for checking spelling. But what about a textbook? They're useful too.
Pietro: **(4)** ....
Valerie: Possibly. Or he may get one free when he pays for the course.
Pietro: **(5)** ....

Use five of these phrases to complete Pietro's part of the conversation.

A Oh yes, that's a good point.
B I don't like them very much.
C Yes they are, but maybe he won't need one because he'll have a teacher.
D Would you like a dictionary or a textbook?
E OK, then afterwards we can decide which one he should buy.
F That's right, and he's only got £20 to spend, so he can't buy all these things, can he?
G Yes, I think he should buy one of those, because it's very useful if you don't know what words mean.

3 **Which two phrases didn't you use? Now listen and check.**

4 **Listening**
- Look at these five sentences.
- Listen to Tim and Janet talking about the courses they are doing in their free time.
- Decide if each sentence is correct or incorrect.
- If you think it is correct, put a tick (✓) in the box under **A** for **YES**. If you think it is not correct, put a tick (✓) in the box under **B** for **No**.

		A YES	B No
1	Janet thinks her computer classes are too long.	☐	☐
2	Tim has learnt many new things on his course.	☐	☐
3	Tim has to buy the food he cooks on his course.	☐	☐
4	Tim asks Janet to help him with his cookery.	☐	☐
5	Janet agrees to help Tim solve a problem.	☐	☐

5 **Writing**

Complete the second sentence so that it means the same as the first, using no more than three words.

1 Each lesson lasts two hours.
Each lesson .... long.
2 What's the price of this CD ROM, please?
How .... this CD ROM cost, please?
3 I think a dictionary is very useful.
A dictionary is very useful .... opinion.
4 I think you are right about the textbook.
I agree .... you about the textbook.
5 Let's talk about the videotape first.
How .... about the videotape first?

All the best books

Read the notices and answer the questions.
- Which one can you probably see in **a)** a library? **b)** a bookshop?
- Which one is **a)** advertising something? **b)** warning you?
- What does each notice mean? Choose **A, B,** or **C**.

1
> Just published -
>
> **Mediterranean Cookery**
> by **Poppy Tobin**
>
> *Signed copies available on request*

A We have published all of Poppy Tobin's books about cooking.

B Sign here if you'd like a copy of Poppy Tobin's latest book.

C Buy a new book with the writer's signature in it here.

2
> Please respect all books in your care.
>
> Heavy fines for any damage to borrowed books.

A Take care when looking at damaged books.

B You'll have to pay if you don't look after our books.

C You can use these books here, but you can't borrow them.

Look at these book covers. What type of book do you think each one is? Choose your answers from the words in the box.

mystery	romance	horror	science fiction
thriller	biography	humour	travel

Which of these books would you like to read? Why do you enjoy this type of book?

A   B   C   D

E   F   G   H

3 Reading

The people in 1–5 all want to buy a book.
- Look at the descriptions of eight books (A–H).
- Decide which one would be most suitable for each person.

1 Laura is looking for a book for her grandson's fifth birthday present. Preferably, it should be about space travel or animals and be a story she can read to him many times.

2 Moira's 14-year-old daughter loves science fiction videos. Moira wants to encourage her to read more by giving her a book which will hold her attention.

3 Fiona, like everyone in her family, is very interested in the cinema and enjoys reading about it. She wants a book that will give her all the gossip about film stars past and present.

4 James, who is 15, is looking for something to pass the time on a long plane journey. He'd like to read an adventure story which brings a period of history to life.

5 Gerry likes mystery stories which are full of suspense and excitement. He'd prefer to buy a book by a new writer.

This week's bargain books

A The Meeting
This exciting novel is aimed at teenagers but adults will enjoy it, too. It's the 16th century and Per, the farm boy, rescues a princess. There are marvellous chases, battle scenes and romantic meetings – you couldn't ask for more thrilling action in a story, or a more realistic picture of the past.

B Stealing Scenes
Starting at the age of five, the writer of this amusing autobiography has had a long and successful career as an actress on stage and screen. She takes us into her world of lights and cameras and tells the secrets of famous people she has known.

C The Bucketful of Dinosaurs
When Harry finds a bucketful of dinosaurs, he's delighted and takes them everywhere he goes until one day he leaves them on a train. How will he prove that the dinosaurs belong to him? Very young children will never get tired of listening to this charming adventure.

D Blood Rain
In this seventh book in the series about an Italian police inspector, the hero investigates a murder. The victim? Maybe just a friendless nobody, or perhaps the son of the country's most powerful criminal. Can the inspector manage both to find the murderer and to stay alive?

E Hex Shadows
This story is set in the year 2367 when Britain is a part of the cruel European Federation. Hexes, human computers who were created in the late 21st century, are now hunted down as enemies of the Federation. This is an exciting, fast-moving story which teenagers will love.

F Space Age
Designed with the fact-hungry child in mind, this gives information about stars, galaxies, astronauts and spaceships. It will bring the universe to life and make science and technology fun for those between five and ten years old.

G Stormy Weather
This thriller is the first from the pen of a young Canadian. It follows the story of Dale, a meteorologist who is invited on a small plane to watch a thunderstorm. Dale soon discovers that not all dangers come from nature, and to save his life he must find the answers to some deadly questions.

H Shoot!
For more than 20 years, this has been recognized as the best guide to the movies. This latest edition gives details and opinions about more than 22,000 films. It tells you about video and DVD availability, which films are suitable for family viewing, and the prizes films have won.

Get ready for PET Reading Part 2

1 Look at the information about Laura. Underline the words that are important about her.
Have you underlined: *grandson's fifth birthday, space travel or animals* and *read... many times*?

2 Which book would be suitable for a child of five (*grandson's fifth birthday*)? Are A, B or E suitable? Why not?
What about C and F? Why? (*very young children, those between five and ten years old*)

3 Are C and F about *space travel* or *animals*? Remember, dinosaurs are animals.

4 C and F can't both be suitable. Which one is unsuitable? Why? So which is the most suitable book for Laura?

5 Now do the same for the other people.

---

4 Vocabulary

Harry had a *bucketful* of dinosaurs. Complete these sentences in an interesting way.

1 Brian can't speak because he's just taken a mouthful of ....
2 You won't get better unless you swallow this spoonful of ....
3 When nobody was looking, Katia gave me a handful of ....
4 Graham felt hungry when he looked at the plateful of ....
5 Jenny's jacket was heavy because she had a pocketful of ....

5 Writing

1 **This is a story called 'The Strange Visitor'. The sentences aren't in the right order. Read the sentences and put them in the correct order. The first one has been done for you.**

☐ She knew what she had to do.
☐ Jenny cried out in surprise and the strange visitor disappeared.
☐ Although the person didn't speak, Jenny could hear some words in her head.
7 One day when Jenny arrived home, she saw someone standing at her front door, hidden underneath a large, old-fashioned coat and hat.
☐ To prepare for that day, you must study hard and learn all you can.'
☐ She went inside, took out her homework and studied all evening.
☐ She didn't know why, but she felt that this person was very old, wise and kind.
☐ 'This is only my first visit, and when we meet again I will show you my home on a distant planet.

2 **Now you are going to write your own story. It is also called 'The Strange Visitor', but it must be a *different* story.**

Before you start to write, answer these questions about your own story.

• Who does the visitor come to see?
• Where and when does the visit happen?
• What is strange about the visitor?
• How does the person visited feel about the visitor?
• What happens in the end?

3 **Write your story in about 100 words.**

3 ① Holiday adventures

1 Reading

Read these notices. Which one can you see a) in a travel agency window? b) at an airport? c) in a hotel?

1

> Find out about
> excursions, nightlife
> and transport to the
> airport at our 24-hour
> reception desk

2

> 70,000 package holidays
> Reservations 9 am - 6 pm
>
> Leave an answerphone
> message outside
> these hours

3

> Do not leave
> your luggage
> unattended
> at any time

What does each notice mean? Choose A, B, or C.

A Make sure there's always someone with your belongings.

B You can make a booking here during the day.

C Someone is always available to give you information.

2 Speaking

1 Look at picture A and answer these questions. Use the words in the box.

1 Who can you see in the picture?
2 Where is she?
3 What's she doing?
4 What things can you see in the picture?
5 How does the girl probably feel? Why?

suitcase	young	wearing	packing
bedroom	nervous	clothes	holiday
quilt	abroad	plastic	woman

A

2 Now use your answers to describe the picture.
Begin: *This picture shows a young woman in her bedroom. She's...*

3 Now look at picture B. Describe what you can see in the picture. Talk about:

• where the picture was taken
• the people
• what they are doing
• the things you can see
• what they are probably talking about

Use these words:

jacket	phone	writing
curly	arrangements	brochures
discussing	travel agency	shelf
desk	trip	pen

B

Begin: *This picture shows two people in a travel agency. They're...*

3 Reading

1 How many of these questions do you answer with 'Yes'?

- Are you interested in wildlife and beautiful scenery?
- Do you enjoy camping?
- Do you prefer to go on holiday with a large group of people?
- Would you like to travel in foreign countries?

If you've answered 'Yes' four times, then you'd probably like the kind of holiday shown below. Do you agree? Why or why not?

2 Read the text to decide if each sentence is correct or incorrect.

1 In a safari truck, passengers take it in turns to sit next to a window.
2 Safari trucks are able to travel over all types of roads.
3 Safari team leaders have a minimum of 12 months' touring experience.
4 The second driver is as experienced as the team leader.
5 Each truck comes supplied with all the food needed for the trip.
6 Everyone is expected to help get meals ready.
7 What people pay for their food depends on how much they eat.
8 There is always enough clean drinking water.
9 Campers have plenty of space in their tents.
10 Hot showers are provided for campers wherever they stop for the night.

Safari Holidays

If you want to get really close to the wildlife and scenery of Africa, then a Safari Holiday offers the most excitement and best value for money.

The Right Trucks for Africa

Each of our safari trucks is a safe, reliable vehicle which is suited to African travel conditions and allows you to fully enjoy the areas visited. Every seat is a window seat and the sides of the truck can be rolled up to provide a wide space for looking out. We use four-wheel-drive vehicles because roads can be rough or get washed away, and we don't want to be prevented from visiting interesting areas.

The Safari Team

Three of our employees go on each safari trip, one of whom is the team leader. All safari team leaders are fully trained and have worked for at least a year on a wide variety of trips in Africa before they lead their first safari. The team leader is a driver, mechanic, guide, diplomat and general expert on Africa. He is helped by a second driver, usually a team leader in training. The third member of the team, the cook, is as important as the leader. He or she sees that all cooking and camp tasks are completed as smoothly as possible.

Good Food

Safari Holidays are famous for their open-fire cooking. We stop regularly to buy fresh fruit, vegetables and meat in local markets and we also have a good supply of things like tea, coffee, dried milk and tinned food in the truck. All the members of the tour lend a hand with the food preparation and washing-up, under the experienced eye of the team cook. At the beginning of each trip, everyone, including the safari team members, pays the same amount of money into the safari purse and this covers food expenses. All water carried on the truck is safe to drink and we make sure it never runs out.

Quality Camping Equipment

Each truck carries everything needed for the trip. This includes four-person tents, used for only two people, air beds, mosquito nets, camp chairs, a fire grill for campfire cooking and all necessary cooking equipment, a cool box for storing fresh food, binoculars, books on Africa and a first-aid kit.

Accommodation

On Safari Holidays, we sometimes camp in an official campsite and sometimes we put up our tents in wild areas. Some campsites have very basic or no facilities, while at others hot showers and cold drinks are available. At the start or finish of tours, we usually have a night in a hotel. These are clean, comfortable and reasonably priced.

1 Don't worry about the meaning of every word. You don't have to understand every word in the text, only the ones which help you do the task.

2 Use the headings to help you find the answers. In which paragraphs can you find the answers to sentences 4, 6, and 9?

3 Underline the words in the text which help you with each sentence. What words will you underline for sentences 1, 3, and 8?

4 Decide if the words in the text and the sentence have the same meaning. Look at number 1. Does *Passengers take it in turns to sit next to a window* mean the same as *Every seat is a window seat*? What about number 2? Does it mean the same as the sentence in the text which begins *We use four-wheel-drive vehicles...* ?

4 Writing

There are several ways to say *when* something happens.

Examples:

*Safari drivers must work for a year **before** they can become team leaders.*
*Safari drivers can become team leaders **after** they have worked for a year.*
*Safari drivers can't become team leaders **until** they have worked for a year.*

***When** the campers have put up their tents, they start cooking dinner.*
*The campers start cooking dinner **as soon as** they have put up their tents.*

*Safari members make a lot of new friends **while** they're on holiday.*
*Safari members make a lot of new friends **during** their holiday.*

Complete the second sentence so that it means the same as the first, using no more than three words.

1 Learn to ski before you go on a winter holiday in the mountains.
Don't go on a winter holiday in the mountains until .... to ski.

2 When we arrived at the hotel, we immediately went for a swim.
We went for a swim as .... we arrived at the hotel.

3 We'll go sightseeing after lunch.
We'll go sightseeing when .... had lunch.

4 During my holiday in Paris, I spoke a lot of French.
I spoke a lot of French while I .... in Paris.

5 Don't book your holiday until you've seen my photos of Africa.
You must see my photos of Africa .... your holiday.

5 Vocabulary

You can use the words in the box when you're talking about holidays. Divide them into the six groups.

~~hotel~~ countryside ~~sunglasses~~ shells plane taking photos ~~swimming~~ coach ~~postcards~~ train guest house ~~car~~ sunbathing tent suntan lotion handicrafts ~~beach~~ guidebook picnics

Transport	Accommodation	Scenery	Activities	Things to pack	Souvenirs
car	hotel	beach	swimming	sunglasses	postcards

Think of words which describe the kind of holiday you like most. Use a dictionary to help you. Add the words to the table.

6 Speaking

Talk about the kind of holidays you like and don't like.

3 2 Just the job

2

1 Reading

Read these messages. What does each one say? Choose A, B or C.

1

E-mail:

....

To: Ronan
From: David

....

Several members of staff are wearing jeans with their uniform jackets, which they know is against company rules. Can you speak to them? Thanks.

2

Ronan,

During the bus strike next week, I can give you a lift to the office. Shall I pick you up at 7 o'clock?

Maddy

The boss wants Ronan to

A inform staff about new company rules.

B ask staff for their opinion of the company uniform.

C warn staff their appearance isn't satisfactory.

What is Maddy offering to do for Ronan?

A drive him to work

B wake him up early

C accompany him on the bus

**Do you think Ronan will be happy to receive these messages?
What kinds of things make people happy or unhappy at work?**

2 Vocabulary

1 Many people have to study for several years before they take up a profession or job. For example, an *architect* has studied *architecture*, and a *doctor* has studied *medicine*. What have these people studied?

Profession	Subject studied
architect	*architecture*
doctor	*medicine*
lawyer	
artist	
cook	
engineer	
tourist guide	
hairdresser	
journalist	
businesswoman	
actor	
chemist	
biologist	
physicist	
musician	

2 Look at these verbs. You can make nouns by changing the end of each one. Complete the table.

Verb	Noun
apply	*application*
organize	
qualify	
decide	
operate	
employ	*employment*
advertise	
govern	
manage	
retire	
insure	
succeed	

Use the pairs of words to make sentences.
Example:
If you want to apply for a job, you have to fill in an application form.

3 Listening **1** You will hear four women talking about their jobs. Listen and complete the information in the table.

Speaker	Clothes	Equipment	Place	Activity
1				*controlling traffic*
2			*advertising agency*	
3		*microscope*		
4				

Listen again and match the speakers with the pictures, A, B, C or D.

A

B

C

D

2 You will hear a woman talking on the radio about her job. Put a tick (✓) in the correct box for each question.

1 Where does Amanda usually work?

A ☐ in a restaurant
B ☐ in her own kitchen
C ☐ in recording studios

2 People are satisfied with
Amanda's service because

A ☐ she provides large meals.
B ☐ she cooks healthy food.
C ☐ she prepares unusual dishes.

3 Amanda finds her job stressful if she

A ☐ has to work in unsuitable places.
B ☐ doesn't know when she should serve a meal.
C ☐ doesn't know how many people to cook for.

4 What does Amanda enjoy most about her job?

A ☐ meeting famous bands
B ☐ working for young people
C ☐ earning a lot of money

5 How does Amanda get to the place where she works?

A ☐ by car
B ☐ by bus
C ☐ on foot

6 When she gets home in the evening, Amanda

A ☐ writes about cooking.
B ☐ cooks for her family.
C ☐ listens to music.

Get ready for PET Listening Part 2

1 Read the questions quickly before you hear the tape, so you know what to listen for.
2 You will hear the recording twice. If you miss the answer to a question, don't worry. Forget that question and think about the next one. You can find the answer when you hear the tape for a second time.
3 The answer to a question may not be in exactly the same words as the ones you hear. For example, what's the answer to question 2? What words does Amanda use to express this idea?

4 For each question, A, B, and C will seem possible, but only one will be right. For example, what is the answer to question 5? Amanda talks about the other kinds of transport, but they are not how she gets to work. What does she say about each kind of transport?
5 Remember to check all your answers when you listen to the tape for a second time.

4 Writing

Write a story which begins with this sentence:

When Mr Boot opened his office door, he knew at once that something was different.

Before you start to write, answer these questions.
- Where did Mr Boot work?
- What was different?
- How did he feel about it?
- What did he do or say about it?
- What happened in the end?

Write your story in about 100 words.

4 ① House and home

1 Vocabulary

1 Which rooms do you have in your house?

dining room	kitchen	bedroom	garage
living room	bathroom	hallway	balcony
garden	stairs	storeroom	basement

Do you have any other rooms in your house?

2 In which room do you usually find these things? Divide them into the four groups. Some words can be used more than once.

dishwasher	wardrobe	chest of drawers	sink
coffee table	washbasin	armchair	dressing table
television	lamp	fridge	shower
cooker	towel rail	mirror	sofa

Living room	Kitchen	Bathroom	Bedroom

2 Speaking

1 In the Speaking test, you talk about a photograph. If you don't know the word for something, you can say what it looks like, or what it is used for.

Example:

What's a coffee table?

It's a small, low table which you usually find in the living room. You can put things like cups of coffee, newspapers and magazines on it.

Talk about these things in the same way:

- a chest of drawers
- a towel rail
- a dishwasher
- a wardrobe
- a vase

2 Choose one of the photographs opposite and describe the room. Use the words in the box to help you talk about:

- the type of room it is
- what you can see in the room
- where the things are
- your opinion of the room
- who you think lives there

> there's a/some
> on top of
> next to/beside
> underneath/below
> to the right of
> to the left of
> behind
> in front of

A

B

3 Listening 🔲 **1** Listen to a boy describing his room. Which room is his?

A ☐ **B** ☐ **C** ☐

2 Describe your house. Talk about:

- where it is
- what it looks like
- how many rooms it has
- your favourite room

4 Writing

Your English penfriend, who's called Chris, has never visited you and has asked you what your room is like.

Write a letter to Chris. In your letter, you should

- tell him how big your room is
- say what is in the room
- explain why you like it

Write 35–45 words.

5 Listening

1 Look at the three pictures. Where is the calculator in each picture? Listen and decide which picture, A, B, or C, matches what you hear.

A ☐   B ☐   C ☐

2 What time does the man's bus leave?

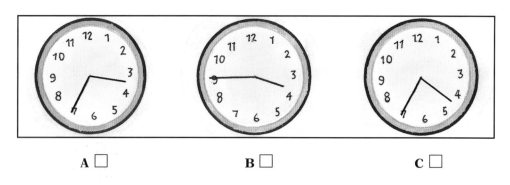

A ☐   B ☐   C ☐

3 What does the woman decide to eat?

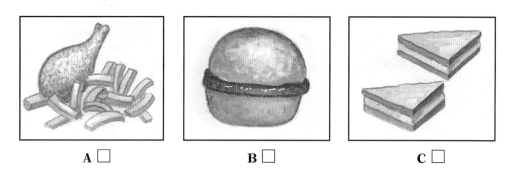

A ☐   B ☐   C ☐

4 Which piece of equipment does the woman need?

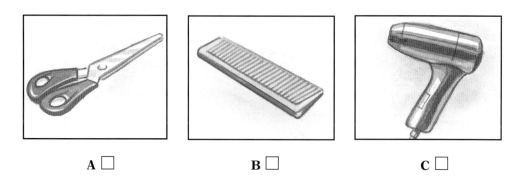

A ☐   B ☐   C ☐

Interesting people

1 Vocabulary

1 How often does your family get together for a celebration? Do you enjoy family parties? Why? Why not?

2 Find someone in the photo who:

is fair-haired	has curly hair	is in blue jeans	is smiling
is middle-aged	looks tired	is wearing glasses	is pointing

Now describe the photo. Begin like this:

'This is a picture of a family party. There are people of all ages here. Most of them are sitting down at a table, but two men...'

3 **The words in the boxes describe people. In the first box, find seven pairs of words with *opposite* meanings.**

attractive	careful	careless	cheerful	confident	miserable	foolish
hard-working	lazy	shy	strong	ugly	weak	wise

4 **In this box, find seven pairs of words with *similar* meanings.**

amusing	anxious	blond	boring	understanding	dull	fair
funny	honest	patient	slim	thin	truthful	worried

5 **Which words describe you?**

2 Writing

You had arranged to meet your cousin at the station, but now you can't go. Write an e-mail to Robin, your English friend. In your e-mail, you should

• ask Robin to meet your cousin for you
• say why you can't go
• describe your cousin

Write 35–45 words.

3 Reading

1 Generally, how old are people when they first a) learn to read? b) go to university? Read the article about a boy who has done these things at a younger age than most people, and then answer the questions.

The most difficult thing for university student Shaun Rogers is opening his classroom door. Shaun can't do this without help because he's only six years old. He's the youngest person ever to study at Rochester University in New York. Shaun began reading at two, and by four was knowledgeable about a range of subjects from astronomy to zoology. By the age of five, he was regularly corresponding with university professors about his ideas. He has just completed his first book which will be published in a few months, shortly after his seventh birthday. 'I love learning,' says Shaun. 'My hero is the scientist Albert Einstein because he never combed his hair or wore socks.'

Psychologists have found it difficult to test Shaun's intelligence because it goes beyond what they usually measure. Shaun's mother first realized her son was different when he kept crying at playschool because he was bored with the children's games. She started teaching him at home after finding that local schools were not prepared for children who learnt at Shaun's speed. Now Shaun is studying geography at Rochester University and using the Internet to complete his high school studies.

However, some psychologists warn that too much study can prevent a child from developing normally. 'I don't care how brilliant the kid is, six-year-olds have to play with their friends,' says Dr Brian Wood. Mrs Rogers disagrees that her son's time is completely taken up by school work. 'He loves the violin and has many outdoor interests, such as camping, fishing and swimming, just like other boys his age.'

1 What is the writer trying to do in the text?
A advise parents about their children's education
B compare the development of normal and clever children
C encourage students to enter university at a young age
D interest people in the life of an unusual child

2 How old was Shaun when he wrote his first book?
A four
B five
C six
D seven

3 Why did Shaun's mother decide to educate him at home?
A because she couldn't find a suitable school for him
B because his school wouldn't let him use the Internet
C because his teachers were unkind and made him cry
D because he didn't get on with the other children

4 What does Dr Wood think about Shaun?
A He isn't really any cleverer than other six-year-olds.
B He should spend more time having fun with other children.
C He will have to study harder to succeed at university.
D He can help his friends to do better at school.

5 Which of these is Mrs Rogers talking about Shaun?

A 'My son gets bored easily if he doesn't have other children to play games or go swimming with him.'

B 'My son loves his studies and fortunately there are many children of his own age in his class who share his interests.'

C 'What makes my son different from other children is that he started studying earlier and learns things much more quickly.'

D 'Like most young boys, my son often looks untidy and spends more time using the Internet than doing his homework.'

Get ready for PET Reading Part 4

1 The first question on this kind of reading text asks you about the writer's purpose. Has the writer of the text about Shaun succeeded in her/his purpose? In other words, has s/he interested you in Shaun's life?

2 In this kind of reading text, you have to understand people's *attitudes* and *opinions* as well as factual information. From this text, what do you understand about:

- Shaun's *attitude* to studying?
- Dr Wood's *opinion* about what six-year-old children need to do?
- Mrs Rogers' *opinion* about the amount of time her son spends studying?

3 In some of the questions in this kind of reading text, you have to look for the answer in more than one place. Look at question 5 and underline the two places in the text which give you the correct answer.

2 **Match the writer's purposes with the sentences.**

1 to recommend something	**A** Couples who decide to adopt a child should be prepared for the time when the child starts to ask difficult questions about the birth parents.
2 to compare two things	**B** Why do people using mobile phones in public places imagine everyone is interested in their conversations and speak in very loud voices?
3 to complain about something	**C** If, like me, you enjoy a film which keeps you sitting on the edge of your seat, then you shouldn't miss this one.
4 to explain something	**D** I felt close to my grandmother because she always met me from school and listened while I described the events of my day.
5 to warn against something	**E** Children with several brothers and sisters may feel differently from an only child when it comes to the school holidays.

4 Writing

Complete the second sentence so that it means the same as the first, using no more than three words.

1 That teacher is very patient with her students.
That is the teacher .... very patient with her students.

2 Shaun is too weak to open the classroom door.
Shaun isn't .... to open the classroom door.

3 In our class, only a few students have curly hair.
In our class, not .... curly hair.

4 My brother prefers funny films to serious ones.
My brother likes funny films .... serious ones.

5 'My favourite film star is Tom Cruise,' said my grandmother.
'Tom Cruise is the film star I like ....,' said my grandmother.

Places of interest

1 Look at the notices, 1–10. Would you find them in a museum, a sports centre, a hotel, a giftshop or a post office?

1
Last collection:
19.30 Mon–Fri.

2
Changing rooms this way

3
Rooms should be vacated by 12.00

4
Ask for our free gift-wrapping service

5
Parcels and heavy items should be taken to window 7 for weighing

6
Please do not touch the exhibits

7
EQUIPMENT
CAN BE HIRED
BY THE HOUR

8
All breakages must be paid for

9
Photocopying facilities are available to guests at Reception

10
A map of the display areas is available at the entrance

2 Look at each notice again. Is it:

a) giving you information about what facilities are available?
b) telling you what you must or mustn't do?
c) giving you simple information, for example where or when?

3 Choose one place from the box below. What type of notices would you expect to see there? Write two examples of each type, a), b) and c).

school	department store	bank	airport

Get ready for PET Listening Part 3

1 In Part 3 of the PET Listening test, you have to listen and write the missing words in the gaps on the question paper.
2 The information on the page may be presented in different ways. Make sure you know what to do. Read the information on the page carefully and think about the type of information that is missing.
3 You don't have to understand every word – just listen for the missing information.
4 You will hear the words you need to write on the tape and you don't need to change them in any way. Don't worry if you're not sure how to spell the words correctly, but make sure you write clearly.
5 Don't write too much. One or two words is usually enough.

1 **Look at the notes about Orford Castle. Some information is missing.**

- You will hear a recorded message about the castle.
- For each question, fill in the missing information in the numbered space.

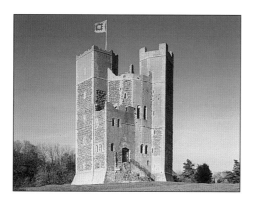

ORFORD CASTLE

Opening time:	(1) ....
Closing time:	4 pm
Price for adults:	£2.30
Price for children:	(2) ....
Telephone number:	(3) 01394 ....

In this example, the words on the left tell you what information you are listening for. Some of the information has already been completed. You only have to fill in the missing information where there is a number in brackets and a dotted line.

2 **Look at the notes about Framlingham Castle. Some information is missing.**

- You will hear a recorded message about the castle.
- For each question, fill in the missing information in the numbered space.

FRAMLINGHAM CASTLE

When it is open:
Between April and (1) ....
Every day from 10.00 am to
(2) ....

What you can do there:
Walk around the (3) ....
Visit the (4) ....

In this example, the information is organized under headings. Again, some of the information is given and you just fill in the missing words.

3 **Look at the notes about Castle Rising. Some information is missing.**

- You will hear a recorded message about the castle.
- For each question, fill in the missing information in the numbered space.

CASTLE RISING

You can visit the castle any day between (1) .... and Sunday.

A free (2) .... gives you information about the castle.

In the giftshop, you can buy a (3) .... as a souvenir.

In this example, information about the castle is given in sentences. Again, some of the information is given, so just fill in the missing words.

3 Reading

Look at the sentences about the trip to Arundel Castle. Read the text and decide if each sentence is correct or incorrect.

1   Arundel Castle is in the same town as the Albion Hotel.
2   If you go on the trip, you may miss your evening meal at the hotel.
3   There is no charge for the journey to Arundel.
4   Arundel Castle is next to the river, in the centre of the town.
5   All of the castle buildings are less than 1,000 years old.
6   Part of the castle is in a poor condition.
7   Part of the castle is used as a private house.
8   It is necessary to book a table if you want to have lunch at the castle.
9   Afternoon tea at the castle is not very expensive.
10   To go on the trip, you have to reserve a place one day in advance.

BRITANNIA HOLIDAYS

Extra trip to Arundel Castle: Wednesday

Dear Holiday-maker,

I hope that you are enjoying your visit to the Albion Hotel. I'm writing to tell you about an extra trip we are arranging for Wednesday afternoon. We'll be going to Arundel Castle, which is a tourist attraction about 40 miles from here. A coach will be leaving at 11 am and returning in time for your evening meal at 7 pm. The kitchen has been informed so if we're late for any reason, they'll wait for us. Please remember this is not part of your package so, although the coach is free, there is an entrance fee of £7.00 if you want to visit the castle.

The town of Arundel is very pretty, with pleasant walks down by the river and some interesting old shops. The castle stands on a hill outside the town and can be seen from miles around. There has been a castle on this site for almost 1,000 years, but the present building is not that old, so it's certainly not an old ruin. The castle buildings are used as a home by the present owners, but quite a large part is open to the public.

Among the things to see at the castle are some lovely rooms. The library has a wonderful ceiling and there is a beautiful bedroom, once used by members of the royal family. There is furniture dating from the 16th century and a fine collection of old clocks, which shouldn't be missed. The picture gallery is also very interesting and has paintings by famous artists such as Canaletto and Gainsborough.

We will arrive in Arundel at lunchtime and the castle has its own restaurant, which serves excellent home-made lunches. If a group of you would like to pre-book, we can arrange a discount for you. If not, you can decide when you arrive and there are always plenty of free tables. For those of you who prefer a lighter meal, traditional English afternoon tea is served in the restaurant from 3.00 pm at a very reasonable price.

So, if you would like to join us on our trip to Arundel, please ask at Reception by Tuesday lunchtime at the latest, and your name will be added to the list.
Have a nice day.

Clara Tongue
Tour Company Representative

4 Speaking

1   **What are the main tourist attractions in your area**
- for young people?
- for older people?
- for foreign visitors?

2   **Talk about a historic building in your country and say what visitors can see and do there.**

5.2 Getting there

5 **2**

1 Look at the words in the box. Divide them into four groups. Some of the words can be used more than once.

driver	pilot	attendant	land	catch	miss
get on	take off	check in	ticket	fare	station
take	platform	boarding pass	meter	timetable	gate

Taxi	Train	Bus/Coach	Plane

2 Complete the gaps in these sentences with words from the table.

1 If we don't hurry up, we'll .... the bus. It leaves the bus .... at ten o'clock.

2 It's cheaper for four people to .... a taxi rather than go on the underground, because the taxi .... comes to less than the price of four ....

3 After you .... your luggage, they give you a .... which you take along to the .... , where someone checks it before you .... the plane.

4 The train to Edinburgh leaves from .... number eight and you have to buy your .... in the office before you ....

5 In the .... , it said that the bus left at 10.00, and so we got there at 09.45 so that we would be sure to .... it.

Look at the photograph and describe it. Make sure you answer these questions:

- Where was it taken? Who are the people? What is each of them doing? Why?
- What things can you see in the photograph?
- What are the people going to do next? Why?

What are the good and bad things about travelling by plane?

3 Reading

1 Look at these notices. On which type of transport would you expect to see each one?

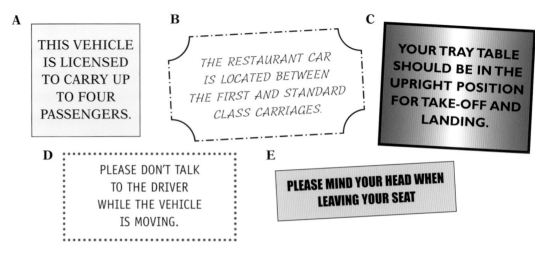

A

THIS VEHICLE IS LICENSED TO CARRY UP TO FOUR PASSENGERS.

B

THE RESTAURANT CAR IS LOCATED BETWEEN THE FIRST AND STANDARD CLASS CARRIAGES.

C

YOUR TRAY TABLE SHOULD BE IN THE UPRIGHT POSITION FOR TAKE-OFF AND LANDING.

D

PLEASE DON'T TALK TO THE DRIVER WHILE THE VEHICLE IS MOVING.

E

PLEASE MIND YOUR HEAD WHEN LEAVING YOUR SEAT

Get ready for PET Reading Part 1

1 In Part 1 of the PET Reading test, there are five multiple-choice (**A**, **B** or **C**) questions.
2 You have to look at either a public notice or a personal message and answer the question about it. The message may be an e-mail or a handwritten note. The notice may be:
- telling you what to do or not to do
- telling you what is available
- giving you information about things

3 This is how to choose the correct explanation:
- First look at the notice or message and imagine how you would explain it to a friend.
- Then look at the three explanations and choose which one is closest to what you would say.
- Finally, check the other explanations and find words and phrases in the notice that tell you that these explanations are incorrect.

2 Look at this notice. Choose the correct explanation, A, B, or C.

Available 1st July.
One-bedroom furnished flat.
Reasonable rent.
Convenient for shops
and buses.

A I'm looking for somewhere to live.

B I'm looking for furniture for a flat.

C I'm looking for someone to live in a flat.

The answer to this question is C.
Which words tell you that this is the answer?
Which words tell you that **A** is not the answer?
Which words tell you that **B** is not the answer?

3 Look at these notices and messages and decide which is the correct explanation, A, B, or C. Think about why your answers are correct and why the others are incorrect.

1

PLEASE SPEAK QUIETLY IN THE LIBRARY AREA. PEOPLE ARE STUDYING NEARBY.

A You are not allowed to talk here.

B You can only stay here if you are studying.

C You should try not to disturb people.

2

Hot and cold snacks served all day.

A   Sit down and a waiter will come to serve you.

B   You can buy drinks here, but not food.

C   You can get a light meal here.

3

E-mail:

To: Yolanda
From: Tina

Did I leave a book in your car? The thing is, it's not mine - I borrowed it from my brother who now wants it back!

What does Tina want Yolanda to do?

A   return the book she borrowed

B   lend her a book

C   look for a book she has lost

4

☎ **Telephone message**

To: Luca

From: Matteo

The football match is going to be on Saturday this week, instead of Sunday. Usual time and place. Everyone else can still play. OK for you?

This week's football match

A   will take place on a different day.

B   will have some different players.

C   will be starting later than usual.

5

ALL VISITORS SHOULD REPORT TO THE OFFICE ON ARRIVAL.

A   Please go to the office before you leave.

B   Please call the office to make an appointment.

C   Please go to the office when you first come here.

4 Writing

You are going to visit an English friend called Jo, who lives in a big city. Send an e-mail to Jo. In your e-mail, you should

- say how you will travel
- tell her what time you will arrive
- say what you'd like to do during your visit

Write 35–45 words.

1 Vocabulary

What's the difference between these pairs of words?
Example:
A jacket is shorter than a coat.
Check your answers in a dictionary.

coat/jacket	shirt/skirt
boot/shoe	socks/tights
tie/belt	wool/cotton
collar/sleeve	spots/stripes
pocket/bag	zip/buttons

2 Reading

Read these notices. Match them with the correct explanation, A, B, C, or D. There is one extra explanation.

1

> **Changing rooms next to lift.**
> **Customers may take in no more than**
> **4 pieces of clothing.**

2

> **Sorry!**
> Lift to women's fashions out of order –
> Use escalator in TV department

3

> **Today only!**
> Prices on all electrical goods greatly reduced

A Because the lift isn't working, you'll have to go upstairs another way.

B You may not change any women's clothes you buy in today's sale.

C If you buy a television today, it will be much cheaper than usual.

D There's a limit to the number of clothes you may try on at one time.

3 Vocabulary

Read the sentences about money and find the missing words in the word square. They are written from top to bottom, left to right, right to left and diagonally.

1 I don't _ _ _ _ a lot of money in my job, but I _ _ _ _ some every week for my holiday.
2 If you don't have cash, you can write a _ _ _ _ _ _ or pay by _ _ _ _ _ _ card.
3 If you don't put that _ _ _ _ in your wallet, and the _ _ _ _ in your pocket, you'll lose them before you can spend them!

C	S	L	S	A	V	E
H	C	H	E	Q	U	E
A	O	R	O	N	X	A
R	I	W	E	P	D	R
G	N	X	E	D	I	N
E	T	O	N	P	I	T
R	E	C	E	I	P	T

4 I got a _ _ _ _ _ _ _ when I bought these books for you, so you can see how much money you _ _ _ me.
5 Some people will borrow money from you, but they'll never _ _ _ _ it to you!
6 People like to _ _ _ _ in big department stores because everything they want is under one roof.
7 How much do you _ _ _ _ _ _ to repair shoes?
8 The service was very good here, so I'm going to leave the waitress a large _ _ _ .

4 Writing

1 In PET Writing Part 3, you may write a letter to an English-speaking friend. Look at this example writing task.

This is part of a letter you receive from an English penfriend.

> *I wanted to buy a T-shirt this morning but I had to go food shopping instead, which I hate. Do you like shopping? Are there any good stores near you?*

Now write a letter answering your penfriend's questions.
Write your letter in about 100 words.

2 **This is the letter one student wrote. Write the missing words.**

Dear Chris,
Thank you **(1)** .... your letter. I agree **(2)** .... you about food shopping. I hate **(3)** ...., too. The supermarket **(4)** .... always crowded and it's boring looking for rice **(5)** .... coffee!
  But I love shopping **(6)** .... clothes even though I **(7)** .... not got much money. My friends and I often **(8)** .... to the shopping centre in my town just to try **(9)** .... clothes. The shop assistants aren't very pleased when **(10)** .... don't buy anything!
  I also enjoy **(11)** .... to a music store in the shopping centre. I **(12)** .... hours there listening to **(13)** .... latest CDs. I always buy something, even if it's only **(14)** .... music magazine.
  Please write to **(15)** .... again soon.
Love,
Angela

- What is the topic of this letter? Is it what the 'English penfriend' wanted to hear about?
- What different kinds of shopping does Angela mention?
- What *reasons* does Angela give for disliking food shopping?
- What *examples* does Angela give of things she does when she's shopping?
- You start a letter with *'Dear...'* followed by a 'hello' sentence. What 'hello' sentence does Angela use?
- You end a letter with a 'goodbye' sentence. What 'goodbye' sentence does Angela use?
- Look at these sentences. Find three 'hello' sentences and four 'goodbye' sentences.
  'Phone me or e-mail me and tell me what you think.'
  'I'm sorry I haven't written for a long time.'
  'I'm looking forward to your next letter.'
  'I was really pleased to hear your news.'
  'Give my best wishes to your family.'
  'It was great to hear from you again.'
  'See you soon.'
- At the end of a letter, you always sign your name. What does Angela write before her signature? Look at these phrases. Find two from an informal letter and one from a formal one.
  Yours sincerely,
  Best wishes,
  Yours,

1 You have a choice in this part of the test. You have to write either a **letter** or a **story**. Read the instructions for both carefully and decide which one you can write best.

2 If you choose to write the **letter**, you will have to reply to something in a letter from an English penfriend. The penfriend's letter will tell you what the topic of your letter should be. Make sure you know what this topic is, eg 'shopping' or 'clothes'. Also make sure that you write about the topic given, and not about something else. Answer any questions your 'penfriend' asks.

3 In your **letter**, start with 'Dear...,' and a 'hello' sentence. You should end with a 'goodbye' sentence, and sign your name.

4 If you choose to write the **story**, you will have either the title or the first sentence to guide you. Ask yourself some questions about your story before you start to write, for example: *Who... ? Where... ? When... ? Why... ? How did ... feel? What happened in the end?*

5 Your **letter** or **story** will look better if you write it in separate paragraphs, as Angela has done. Start each paragraph on a new line.

6 Try not to write fewer than 100 words, but don't write many more than 100.

7 When you've written your **letter** or **story**, check it carefully. Correct any grammar or spelling mistakes.

3 Write this letter.
This is part of a letter you receive from an English penfriend.

> I wore new shoes to a party last night and now my feet hurt. I hate wearing uncomfortable clothes! Tell me about the clothes you like and don't like wearing. What do you wear to parties?

Now write a letter telling your penfriend about the clothes you like.
Write your letter in about 100 words.

5 Listening

Do you like shopping in street markets? Why? Why not?
- Look at the advertisement for some street markets in London.
- Some information is missing.
- Listen to the man talking on the radio about the markets, and fill in the missing words.

East London Markets

Columbia Road
Over 50 stalls selling (1) .... at bargain prices.

Brick Lane
A market speciality is (2) ....

Petticoat Lane
Sells everything from clothes to toys. Busiest day is (3) ....

Whitechapel
It's opposite (4) ....
Get your Asian vegetables and spices here.

Come and be part of the fun!

6 ② City life

1 Look at these photographs. Choose one of the photographs and make a list of all the things you can see. Use the ideas to help you.

A  B

people

colours

objects

clothes

parts of the
vehicle

buildings

2 Answer these questions about your photograph.

1 What type of vehicle is it?
2 What type of street is it?
3 What are the people in the photo doing?
4 Why are they doing it?
5 How do you think they feel about it?

3 Now look at the other photograph and answer these questions.

1 What's the same or similar?
2 What's different?

1 Which is better, living in a city or living in the country? Why?

2 Look at the adjectives in the box. Which would you use to describe
a) living in the city? b) living in the country?

calm	crowded	peaceful	clean	noisy
dirty	boring	relaxing	stressful	convenient
expensive	exciting	safe	lonely	interesting
fun	dangerous	polluted	inconvenient	

3 Make lists of the advantages of living in a) the city and b) the country.
Use the words in the box to help you.

shopping	night-life	fresh air	way of life	education
employment	transport	health	entertainment	

4 **Talk to another student. Decide who is Student A and who is Student B. Use your lists to have a discussion about life in the two places. Use some of the expressions below.**

Student A
Try to convince your partner that the city is the best place to live.

Student B
Try to convince your partner that the country is the best place to live.

One big (dis)advantage of the city/country is that...

But we have to remember that it is easier to ...... in the city/country.

Don't forget that the city/country is much more ...... than the country/city.

Another thing is that the city/country is better for...

I'm afraid I don't agree with you because...

Yes, you're right, but I still think...

Get ready for PET Speaking Part 3

1   In Part 3 of the PET Speaking test, you have to talk about a photograph which shows an everyday situation.
2   You have to tell the examiner what you can see in the picture. You talk for less than a minute.
3   Remember:
- start immediately, and keep talking – don't stop and think.
- talk to the examiner, not your partner.
- talk about everything you can see.

- if you don't know the word for an object in the photograph, say what it looks like, or what it is used for.
- don't stop if you can't think of the word you need; talk about something else in the photograph.
- listen when your partner is talking.

5 **When you talk about the photograph, use these ideas to help you.**

1 Talk about the *place* in the photograph.
- Is it indoors or outdoors?
- Is it in a house or another building?
- What type of place is it?

2 Talk about the *people* in the photograph.
- How many people are there?
- What do they look like?
- What are they wearing?
- How do they feel?

3 Talk about *what's happening* in the photograph.
- What are the people doing?
- Why are they doing it?

6 **Look at the photograph of some people in the countryside. Talk about it using the ideas in 5.**

7 **Look at the photograph of people in a city and talk about it. Remember:**
- don't talk for more than one minute
- talk about everything you can see in the picture
- don't worry about words you don't know

8 **Talk about a city you know. Say what you like about it and what you don't like about it.**

1 Look at the foods in the box. Divide them into the four groups.

carrots	beans	lamb	peas	onions	garlic
mushrooms	bananas	sausages	grapes	tomatoes	oranges
duck	pasta	beef	rice	chicken	leeks
olives	mayonnaise	tuna	butter	cheese	spinach
pepper	salt	steak	pizza	plums	burgers

Meat and fish	Vegetables	Fruit	Other

2 Add your favourite foods to the lists.

1 Choose one of the photographs of people eating and talk about it. Remember to talk about everything you can see, including:
- each person – what they are doing, wearing and feeling
- the food and drink
- other things in the foreground
- things in the background

A

B

2 What is your favourite food? Talk about:

- breakfast
- dinner
- a snack
- a special meal
- a special treat

What do you drink with these foods?

Get ready for PET Speaking Part 4

1 In Part 4 of the PET Speaking test, you have a conversation with your partner. You only have a few minutes for the task.

2 The examiner tells you what to talk about, but does not ask you any questions.

3 The topic of Part 4 is the same as the one in the pictures in Part 3.

4 Remember:
- talk to your partner, not to the examiner
- ask your partner questions
- listen and respond to what your partner says
- don't talk for too long, and give your partner a chance to speak.

3 Look at the photographs again and listen to the examiner's instructions for the Part 4 task. What is the topic of the conversation? Make a list of the things you can talk about and the questions you can ask your partner. Think about how to begin the conversation.

Have the conversation with another student.

4 Listen to two students beginning the task. As you listen, think about:
- how they begin
- how long each person speaks for
- how they show interest in what each other says

5 Work with another student and do this Part 4 task. Don't talk for too long without involving your partner! Remember to ask questions and show interest. Use some of these phrases.

That's interesting because...

I like ...... , don't you?

I agree with you about that.

Really?

So do I!

Me too, and another thing is...

What about you?

Talk together about good restaurants you have been to and what you like to eat there.

3 Vocabulary

1 Look at the recipe and picture. Can you complete the gaps in the list of ingredients?

some different-sized ....
a small tin of ....
two spoonfuls of ....

a hard-boiled ....
some black ....
two spoonfuls of ....

What equipment do you think you need to make this recipe?

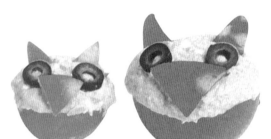

Now listen and check your ideas.

2 How do you think you make this recipe? Use these verbs and the ingredients above to talk about it.

cut	mix	stir
pour	take out	

First you have to...

Then you...

Finally you...

Now listen and check your ideas. Complete the table as you listen.

	Equipment	Verb	Ingredients
1			
2			
3			
4			
5			
6			
7			

4 Writing

Complete the second sentence so that it means the same as the first, using no more than three words.

1 In our house, the salad is usually prepared by my brother.
In our house, my brother .... the salad.
2 At breakfast, all the orange juice was finished.
At breakfast, someone .... orange juice.
3 My mother said: 'Don't burn the rice!'
My mother told .... burn the rice.
4 In the restaurant, Robbie asked for a burger and chips.
In the restaurant, Robbie said: 'Can .... a burger and chips, please?'
5 Martine suggested we ordered a pizza.
Martine said: 'Let's .... a pizza.'

7 ②

Your own space

Speaking

Talk about how important each of these things is for you at home:
1 a room or space which is your own
2 a quiet place where you can relax or study
3 a place where you can make as much noise as you like
4 a place where you can invite your friends in comfort
5 your own special seat at the dining table
6 somewhere outside, for example a balcony or garden

Reading

1 **Read this text about teenagers. Choose the correct word, A, B, C or D, for each space.**

PERSONAL SPACE

More and more people live in large cities these days and this means that it is becoming more and more difficult to find space and time for ourselves. But for many people, personal privacy is very important. In many homes, a few minutes in the bathroom is all the privacy that is **(1)** ....

Teenagers especially need their own personal space at home where they can feel relaxed and private. But, of course, not all teenagers are **(2)** .... enough to have a room of their own. Where space is short, they often have to **(3)** .... a bedroom with a brother or sister. In that case, it's a good **(4)** .... for them to have a special area or corner of the room to **(5)** .... their own. It's especially important for young people to have somewhere to **(6)** .... their personal things. This may or may not be a tidy place and it is not a good idea for parents to try and tell teenagers how to **(7)** .... their space as this is **(8)** .... to lead to arguments. Parents can, however, **(9)** .... sure that there are enough storage spaces such as shelves, cupboards and boxes. This will **(10)** .... the teenager to keep their space tidy if they want to.

1	**A** confident	**B** available	**C** general	**D** average
2	**A** dizzy	**B** early	**C** lucky	**D** happy
3	**A** separate	**B** share	**C** divide	**D** join
4	**A** sense	**B** opinion	**C** idea	**D** thought
5	**A** mind	**B** call	**C** say	**D** tell
6	**A** belong	**B** save	**C** support	**D** keep
7	**A** organize	**B** repair	**C** operate	**D** review
8	**A** really	**B** quickly	**C** actually	**D** likely
9	**A** find	**B** make	**C** get	**D** put
10	**A** afford	**B** let	**C** allow	**D** set

2 Read the complete text again and answer these questions.

1 What is the writer trying to do in this text?
A complain about something
B blame someone for something
C give advice about something
D warn people about something

2 What does the writer believe?
A Teenagers can be selfish.
B Everybody needs some privacy.
C Parents can be unreasonable.
D Sharing is more important than privacy.

3 What does the writer think about tidiness?
A It is important for teenagers to be tidy.
B It is possible even when space is limited.
C It's a waste of time trying to be tidy.
D Parents should make their children be tidy.

3 Listening

Get ready for PET Listening Part 4

1 Part 4 of the PET Listening test is always a conversation between two people. They will be giving their opinions about something, and agreeing or disagreeing with each other.

2 Remember to read the instructions carefully to find out:
- who is talking
- where they are
- what they are talking about.
This will help you to imagine the situation and understand what they say.

3 Remember to read the sentences on the question paper carefully to:
- make sure you know whose opinion the sentence is about
- check if the sentence matches the text or not.

4 You may not understand all the words in the text. Don't worry, you only have to answer six questions with YES or NO. If you're not sure, guess. You have a 50 per cent chance of being right!

1 Read the instructions for this Part 4 task.
- Look at the six sentences for this part.
- You will hear a conversation between a man, Bob, and a woman, Mary. They are talking about their teenage children.
- Decide if you think each sentence is correct or incorrect.
- If you think it is correct, put a tick (✓) in the box under **A** for **YES**. If you think it is incorrect, put a tick (✓) in the box under **B** for **NO**.

2 Now listen and complete the task.

	A YES	B No
1 Mary's house is too small for Matthew to have his own room.	☐	☐
2 Matthew is a lot younger than his brother.	☐	☐
3 Bob wanted to spend more time alone as a teenager.	☐	☐
4 Matthew would like to have his own computer.	☐	☐
5 Mary feels that Matthew's brother has more need of a computer.	☐	☐
6 Matthew would like to watch the television more.	☐	☐

4 Speaking

What do you think?
1   How do you organize your personal space?
2   Do people respect your personal space?
3   Do you respect other people's space?
4   Do you think that tidiness is important?

5 Listening

Now do this task.
- Look at the six sentences.
- Alice and Harry are talking about their personal space.
- As you listen, decide if each sentence is correct or incorrect.
- If you think it is correct, put a tick (✓) in the box under **A** for **YES**. If you think it is incorrect, put a tick (✓) in the box under **B** for **NO**.

		A YES	B NO
1	Alice regrets arguing with her mother.	☐	☐
2	Alice thinks her mother should put clothes away for her.	☐	☐
3	Alice tidies her room when she's expecting visitors.	☐	☐
4	Alice's wardrobe is too small for all her clothes.	☐	☐
5	Harry sometimes lets his brother wear his clothes.	☐	☐
6	Harry and his brother have to share a bedroom.	☐	☐

6 Speaking

Look at the two photographs. Talk about what you can see in each room.

A

B

8 1 Close to nature

1 Vocabulary

Use the words in the box to complete this text about the environment.
Write one word in each space.

| breathe | destroying | dusty | fuels | inhabitants | minerals |
| poverty | prevent | rescue | rubbish | spoil | urgent |

STOP DAMAGING THE EARTH!

We have spent the last one hundred years **(1)** .... our environment. In cities, factories and cars
pollute the air we **(2)** .... , and everything we touch is **(3)** .... and dirty. We **(4)** .... the
countryside by throwing away our **(5)** .... there, and ruin areas of natural beauty by digging up
(6) .... , such as iron and gold, and **(7)** .... , such as coal and oil. While some people get rich,
others suffer from **(8)** .... , hunger and disease. We must **(9)** .... this situation from getting
worse. Finding a way to **(10)** .... our planet is an extremely **(11)** .... problem for all the
(12) .... of the world.

2 Listening

1 Last Saturday three people went out for the day. They each took a photograph.

A   B   C

Listen to the three people talking about the weather on their day out and decide
which photo each person took.

Speaker 1 ....   Speaker 2 ....   Speaker 3 ....

2 Listen to the three speakers again and write down all the weather words
they use.

Good weather	Bad weather	Other weather words
fine	storms	forecast

3 Speaking

Talk about:
- weather that makes you feel cheerful/depressed
- clothes you wear in different kinds of weather
- activities you do in different kinds of weather
- the weather and holidays, celebrations and sports events

48

4 Reading

Read this text about giraffes. Choose the correct word, A, B, C or D, for each space.

THE GIRAFFE

Giraffes are the tallest of all animals. When it is born, a baby giraffe **(1)** .... about 1.7 metres and it grows to 5.3 metres in height. The giraffe has a strong and **(2)** .... long tongue (40 cm) which it uses to **(3)** .... leaves off trees. A giraffe **(4)** .... most of the water it needs from leaves and so it can go for more than a month **(5)** .... drinking. When it has a drink, it has to stand with its front legs wide apart in order to **(6)** .... the water. If it needs to **(7)** .... itself, it does so by kicking, but it has **(8)** .... enemies. A lion may jump on a giraffe if one passes under the tree **(9)** .... the lion is sitting, but giraffes have such good eyesight they usually **(10)** .... the lion in time.

1	**A** measures	**B** weighs	**C** looks	**D** appears
2	**A** greatly	**B** much	**C** extremely	**D** too
3	**A** put	**B** carry	**C** bring	**D** tear
4	**A** holds	**B** gets	**C** picks	**D** keeps
5	**A** except	**B** until	**C** through	**D** without
6	**A** reach	**B** arrive	**C** come	**D** move
7	**A** fight	**B** defend	**C** strike	**D** attack
8	**A** little	**B** any	**C** few	**D** other
9	**A** which	**B** where	**C** how	**D** that
10	**A** notice	**B** realize	**C** mind	**D** watch

Get ready for PET Reading Part 5

1 First read through the whole text to get a good idea of the general meaning.
2 Sometimes your knowledge of *vocabulary* is tested, for example in 4. Only one of these verbs (*holds, gets, picks, keeps*) makes sense in this sentence. Try each one in the space before you decide which is the correct word.
3 Sometimes your knowledge of *grammar* is tested, for example in 8. Only one of these words (*little, any, few, other*) is correct here. Which one? Why are the other words incorrect?
4 Sometimes your knowledge of *vocabulary and grammar* is tested, for example in 6. The four words (*reach, arrive, come, move*) have similar meanings but only one is correct here. Which one? If you put *arrive, come* or *move* in the space, what other words would you need to make the sentence correct?

5 Listening 🔊 You will hear someone talking on the radio about some animals and the extraordinary things that happened to them. Put a tick [✔] against the correct answer for each question.

1 How far did Daisy, the cow, fly on her first flight?
  A ☐ across the road
  B ☐ across a field
  C ☐ 2 km

2 What kind of transport does Speedy, the cat, use?
  A ☐ motorbike
  B ☐ car
  C ☐ bicycle

3 Who finally caught Fluffy, the cat, in the plane?
  A ☐ the pilot
  B ☐ a flight attendant
  C ☐ her owner

4 When does Tom worry about his pigeon, Pete?
  A ☐ when he's going fast
  B ☐ when cars are overtaking
  C ☐ when he's turning right

5 What did Rambo, the gorilla, do when the boy cried?
  A ☐ He held his hand.
  B ☐ He touched his face.
  C ☐ He made noises.

6 What had happened to the boy before Prince, the dog, found him?
  A ☐ He was buried by snow.
  B ☐ He had fallen down a mountain.
  C ☐ He had fallen out of a tree.

6 Speaking

Discuss these questions.
1 Someone wants to give you an animal as a pet. Which one will you choose? Why?

goldfish	kitten	duck	rabbit	mouse	monkey

2 Which of these animals do you think helps humans most? Why?

bee	chicken	cow	elephant	horse	dog

3 Which of these animals would you be most afraid to meet? Why?

spider	snake	shark	bat	tiger	bear

7 Writing

This is part of a letter you receive from an English penfriend.

> I went horse-riding yesterday morning, and then I watched a brilliant TV programme about dolphins. I love all animals! How about you? Have you got a pet?

Now write a letter answering your penfriend's questions.
Write your letter in about 100 words.

1 Reading

1 **Would you like to tour a foreign country on a bicycle? Which countries do you think it would be good to visit in this way? Would tourists enjoy travelling through your country by bike?**

2 **Read the sentences about cycling in Sri Lanka. Then read the text and decide if each sentence is correct or incorrect.**

1 More people in Sri Lanka ride a mountain bike than any other kind of bike.
2 The writer says that you can go a satisfactory distance each day on a bike.
3 The writer says a bicycle is a restful way of travelling through Sri Lanka.
4 The canals provide water for rice growing in spaces in the jungle.
5 The writer admired the colours of the countryside.

On two wheels in a green land

It is often said that the best way to see a country is to use the method of transport which is traditional in that particular place. So people should see Argentina on horseback, Nepal on foot and the US by car. If this is true, then a bicycle is the perfect way to visit Sri Lanka. Although the 18-speed mountain bike I used is not an everyday sight, more traditional models are popular all over the country.

Sharing the same kind of transport as local people changes the way you see the place. You are travelling at a speed that somehow fits the scenery – not so slow that you only see a small area each day, and not so fast that the details of the countryside are missed. Better still, you can stop whenever you want to listen to the birds or a waterfall, talk to people, smell their cooking or take a photo. However, this doesn't mean cycling in Sri Lanka is relaxing. If you want to see the whole country, you have to leave the towns and villages and cycle through jungle, where the temperature is 37 degrees, cross streams, climb hills and go over paths which are made of mud, rock or sand.

The most pleasant paths in the jungle follow the irrigation canals. These carry water into the bright green rice fields which appear at regular intervals among the trees. During the afternoon, groups of children, farm workers and water buffalo all come to swim in the canals. Then, when you climb from the jungle up into the hilly area in the centre of the country, you see every hillside is covered with neat rows of tea bushes in another brilliant shade of green. In fact, the whole country is covered in more different and beautiful shades of green than I ever thought possible.

Now I'm wondering where to ride my bike next – perhaps alongside the canals of The Netherlands, or through the city streets of China...

2 Vocabulary

Look at these groups of words. Which one is different? Why?
Example:
sea   ocean   bush   lake
bush *is different because it's not water.*

1 mountain   desert   cliff   hill
2 waterfall   country   continent   district
3 forest   wood   jungle   island
4 stream   canal   cave   river
5 bay   mud   sand   soil
6 path   road   track   wave
7 valley   coast   shore   beach
8 border   flood   frontier   edge

3 Speaking

Do you like adventure films? What difficulties and dangers do the heroes meet?
Who do you want to win in this kind of film – the heroes or the villains?
Imagine this situation.

• A famous director of adventure films wants your advice about the location of his next film. Here are some places where the action in the film may happen.

• Talk about the adventures the hero and heroine may have in each place and say which you think will be the most exciting.
• Which actors would you like to star in this film? Do you think it would be a popular film?

4 Writing

1 Here are some sentences about geography. Complete the second sentence so that it means the same as the first, using no more than three words.

1 Britain is an island, so everywhere is near to the sea.
Britain is an island, so nowhere is .... the sea.

2 Never walk in the desert without taking water with you.
Take water with you if you're .... a walk in the desert.

3 Look at a map of the Indian Ocean if you want to find Sri Lanka.
You won't find Sri Lanka unless .... a map of the Indian Ocean.

4 I became a geography teacher five years ago.
I .... a geography teacher for five years.

5 The geography teacher asked if they wanted to watch a video.
The geography teacher said, 'Would .... watch a video?'

2 Now look at these sentences about going to live in a different country. Complete the second sentence so that it means the same as the first, using no more than three words.

1 Yesterday, our passport photos were taken by a photographer.
Yesterday, a photographer .... our passport photos.

2 My suitcases are heavier than my brother's.
My brother's suitcases aren't .... mine.

3 At first, we'll have difficulty understanding the language.
At first, understanding the language will be .... us.

4 We have to find a flat before we can look for a school.
We can't look for a school until we .... a flat.

5 My brother and I have both promised to send e-mails to our friends.
I've promised to send e-mails to my friends and .... my brother.

Get ready for PET Writing Part 1

1 This part is a test of your grammar. Everything you write must be correct.
2 The second sentence *must* have the same meaning as the first sentence.
3 There are several different kinds of changes that you have to make. For example:
- find words with the opposite meaning. (1.1)
- change the order of the words. (1.2)
- change the tense of the verb. (1.4)
- change reported speech to direct speech. (1.5)
- make a passive sentence into an active one. (2.1)
- change the way you compare two things. (2.2)
4 Remember you may have to write one, two or three words in your answer. Never write more than three words. Contractions (eg *don't, I've*) count as two words.

5 Reading

Look at the messages. What does each one say? Choose A, B or C.

1
> **To:** Tyler
> **From:** Liza
> ....
> Can you record the programme about the world's oceans at 8.00 pm for me? I forgot to set the video before leaving home. Thanks.

A Liza wants to make sure she doesn't miss a television programme.

B Liza wants Tyler to get a video for them to watch this evening.

C Liza wants Tyler to stay at home until a television programme finishes.

2
> To Class 6B
> Your projects on Antarctica are due in on Monday. Still need help? Then try the websites on the list on the noticeboard.
> Mrs Barton

A Mrs Barton will see students who need help with their projects on Monday.

B Mrs Barton would like students to help her with a website about Antarctica.

C Mrs Barton says websites may help students finish their work on time.

Free time

1 Vocabulary

1 Rearrange these letters to make the names of sports.

Example:

TALLBOFO = football

1	FRIWGUSNNID	**5**	DOJU
2	BLATTNIESEN	**6**	COKYEH
3	FLOG	**7**	SEALLABB
4	STYGNIMCAS		

2 Which of these sports do you like playing? What equipment do you need? Which of these sports do you like watching? What skills must the players have?

2 Reading

What do you like to do in your school holidays?

- These people are all looking for a school holiday activity.
- Read the descriptions of eight school holiday activities on page 55.
- Decide which activity (letters **A–H**) would be most suitable for each person (numbers **1–5**).

1 Gwen is 18 and wants to take her younger brothers and sisters, aged between eight and 15, somewhere where they can get close to animals. She's just failed her driving test.

2 Matthew would like to take his daughter somewhere special on her sixth birthday, but he's only free in the afternoon. She loves hearing stories about animals but is frightened of real ones.

3 Lindsey has 11-year-old twin boys who hate sitting still. She wants to take them somewhere they can enjoy themselves safely all day while she goes to work.

4 Lewis is 15 and wants to do something exciting for the day with some friends from the school swimming team. They're keen to do something connected with either music or sport.

5 Jenny's going to look after her grandchildren, aged ten and seven, for the day. She can't afford to spend any money, but she'd like them to have some entertainment before she takes them home for lunch.

Holiday Fun
for Young People

A Pineapple Theatre Every day at 3 o'clock, young children (4–7 years) can watch 'Stardog'. The fun dog from space invents things to help earth people. At 5 o'clock, a group of 10–16-year-olds presents 'Football Fever', a play about young sports stars. All tickets £3.

B Queen's Arts Centre A day-long course for children (9–13 years) introduces the art of telling stories through music and poetry. Use your own history to make a musical piece. Younger children (4–8 years) may use rubbish to make musical instruments and then play them. No charge for entrance.

C Museum Gardens Circus skills workshop for children (7–11 years). Try juggling, rope walking and putting on clown make-up. Or watch Tiptop Theatre tell the story of a Native American boy and his horse. Both programmes 10–12 am. Entrance free.

D Sunshine Safari We have three floors of slides, swings, rope bridges and other adventure activities. Young adventurers can join a tiger hunt or swim with crocodiles. It all seems very real! Leave your children (3–14 years) in the care of our trained staff. £35 per day, lunch extra.

E Balloon flight See the countryside without having to drive! Our gas-filled balloon is tied to the ground and doesn't actually travel, but the views are fantastic. Price: £12 adult, £7.50 child. No under 5s, no children under 16 without an adult.

F Sea Life Centre Discover facts about life under the sea and watch many varieties of fish. The three-hour tour includes handling starfish, feeding sharks and swimming with dolphins. Adults £4.95, children £3.50.

G Making waves This adventurous programme for 12–18-year-olds gives you a chance to try your skills in a sailing boat, a canoe and a motor boat for just £12 a day. Full instruction is given. You must be a good swimmer and agree to follow all safety rules.

H Paradise Animal Park Drive your car through the park and get close to some of the world's most beautiful and dangerous animals. Younger visitors can have fun in the play area, while there is excitement for older children in the adventure playground with its 10-metre free-fall slide. Family ticket £25.

Get ready for PET Reading paper

1 You have 1 hour and 30 minutes for the Reading and Writing paper. Plan your time carefully.
2 There are five reading parts to the paper. Each part has a different kind of reading text with its own questions.
3 You can get 35 marks for the Reading paper, one mark for each question.
4 In the exam you get a question paper and an answer sheet (see p.92-3). You can make notes on the question paper but you must mark all your answers on the answer sheet.
5 You must use pencil on the answer sheet. Take a pencil, pencil sharpener and rubber to the exam.
6 Read the texts carefully, but don't worry if there are words you don't understand. You probably don't need to know them to answer the questions.
7 Mark one letter for each question. To make a change, rub it out carefully and mark the new answer clearly.
8 If there is a question you can't answer, leave it and go back to it later.
9 Near the end of the test time, check your answers and make sure you have marked an answer for everything. If you don't know something, guess – you may be right!
10 There is more information about this paper in the **Get ready** boxes in this book. Make sure you read them again before the exam.

3 Vocabulary

1 These people are all planning to do their favourite free-time activity. What does each person need? Choose the words from the box.

I'm going to make a skirt to wear to the party tomorrow.

I'm going to decorate my bedroom and put up some shelves.

I'm going to answer this letter from my penfriend.

I'm going to do some work in the garden.

I'm going to have a game of tennis.

1   2   3   4   5

balls	brush	dictionary	envelope	flower pot	net
hammer	material	nails	needle	notepaper	
racket	paint	scissors	pins	watering can	
seeds	spade	sports bag	stamp	refreshing drink	

2 What's your favourite free-time activity? What do you need to do it?

4 Speaking

A friend of yours has just moved to a different town and wants to take up a hobby that will help him/her make new friends. Here are some pictures of some hobbies he/she could do.

- Talk about how interesting the different hobbies are, and decide which will be best for making friends.

Get well soon!

1 Writing

1 Do you think you have a healthy lifestyle? What makes your lifestyle healthy or unhealthy?

2 You and your English friend, Alex, have decided to have a more healthy lifestyle.
Write an e-mail to send to Alex. In your e-mail, you should

• tell Alex about your new sleeping habits
• say what type of food you plan to eat in future
• suggest some exercise or sport you can do together

Write 35–45 words.

2 Vocabulary

Read the sentences about health and sickness and find the missing words in the word square. They are written from top to bottom, left to right, right to left and diagonally.

1 This is an _ _ _ _ _ _ _ _ _ ! Some people have been hurt in a road _ _ _ _ _ _ _ _ , and they need an _ _ _ _ _ _ _ _ _ to take them to hospital.

2 I have bad _ _ _ _ _ _ _ so the doctor sent me to the ear _ _ _ _ _ _ at the hospital. Now I have to take a _ _ _ _ three times a day to make the _ _ _ _ go away.

3 A _ _ _ _ person can't hear without the help of a hearing aid.

4 A doctor and a _ _ _ _ _ both work in a hospital. A _ _ _ _ _ _ _ is a sick person they look after.

5 Even if we had a _ _ _ _ to cure every disease, would everyone be _ _ _ and healthy?

6 Doctor, I feel really _ _ _ . I've got a cold, a _ _ _ _ throat, and a high temperature. And just listen to my horrible _ _ _ _ _ ! I think I've got _ _ _ .

7 When I cut myself with a bread knife, the _ _ _ _ _ was quite deep. There was a lot of blood so my face went _ _ _ _ , I felt _ _ _ _ _ and thought I was going to fall over, but fortunately I didn't _ _ _ _ _ .

A	M	B	U	L	A	N	C	E
C	L	I	N	I	C	U	P	M
C	S	E	H	C	A	R	A	E
I	O	Q	P	J	P	S	T	R
D	R	U	G	I	A	E	I	G
E	E	K	G	F	L	U	E	E
N	I	A	P	H	E	L	N	N
T	T	I	F	A	I	N	T	C
W	O	U	N	D	I	Z	Z	Y

3 Reading

Read the text and questions. For each question, decide which is the correct answer, A, B, C or D.

TV

"I'm sure I'm not the only person my age (15) who hates going to the dentist. Channel 4's late-night documentary *Open wide* last Tuesday was excellent for people like me. However, none of my school friends watched it. They missed this opportunity to see something interesting and educational because the programme didn't appear in the *TV Guide*. This was a pity, as it was the type of programme that makes both young people and their parents think about things they don't normally consider. Why can't television companies let us know about such important documentaries in advance?

This programme was important because it showed how methods for helping people with toothache have developed over the centuries. If you think visiting the dentist today is an uncomfortable experience, just be grateful you didn't live 200 years ago! Then, the programme told us, the only cure for toothache was removing the tooth. There weren't any dentists, so the person who cut your hair also pulled out your bad teeth, and there was nothing to stop you feeling the pain.

The programme has also completely changed my attitude to looking after my teeth. My parents were always saying to me things like, 'Don't eat too many sweets,' and, 'Brush your teeth after meals,' but I never paid much attention. Now I've seen what damage sugar can do, especially if I don't use a toothbrush regularly, I'm going to change my habits. Many people would benefit from a repeat of this programme."

Sophie Ashley, Oxford

1 Why has Sophie written this letter?
A to complain about the time a television programme was shown
B to ask for more television programmes designed for school children
C to advise people to watch a particular television programme
D to persuade a television company to show a programme again

2 Why didn't Sophie's school friends see *Open wide*?
A They didn't know it was on.
B They don't enjoy that type of programme.
C Their parents wouldn't let them.
D It wasn't shown on a channel they can receive.

3 What did *Open wide* say about toothache?
A In the past, nobody could make it stop.
B Dentists used to help people who had it.
C Hairdressers have it more than other people.
D Ways of curing it have changed.

4 What does Sophie think about her parents now?
A They don't know as much as her about teeth.
B Their advice is worth listening to.
C They eat things which are bad for them.
D They don't clean their teeth often enough.

5 Which of these gives information about the programme Sophie watched?

A A play about a 19th-century dentist and how he brought comfort to his patients.

B The series about health care for teenagers. This week, good eating habits.

C This history of the dentist's profession shows what happens when we eat.

D We suggest how to prepare young children for that first visit to the dentist.

4 Writing

Complete the second sentence so that it means the same as the first, using no more than three words.

1 Last night, I took an aspirin to stop my head aching.
  Last night, I took an aspirin because .... aching.
2 My brother goes jogging because he must keep fit for his job.
  My brother goes jogging to .... for his job.
3 If you don't give up coffee, you'll never sleep well.
  You'll never sleep well unless .... coffee.
4 People with flu should stay in bed for a few days.
  Stay in bed for a few days if you .... flu.
5 Smoking isn't allowed in hospitals.
  You .... in hospitals.

5 Writing

Write one of the following questions.

1 **This is part of a letter you receive from an English penfriend.**

I've got flu. I feel terrible and I'm bored because I have to stay in bed. What can I do to make myself feel more cheerful? Tell me about the last time you were ill.

Now write a letter answering your penfriend's questions.
Write your letter in about 100 words.

2 **Your English teacher has asked you to write a story.**
This is the title for your story:
A cure for toothache

Write your story in about 100 words.

Get ready for PET Writing paper

1 You have 1 hour and 30 minutes for the Reading and Writing paper. The writing comes at the end of the paper so plan your time carefully.
2 There are three writing parts to the paper: completing sentences, writing a short message and writing a letter or story.
3 You can get 25 marks for the Writing paper: 5 marks for Part 1, 5 marks for Part 2 and 15 marks for Part 3.
4 In the exam, you get a question paper and an answer sheet (see p.92-3). You can make notes on the question paper but you must write your answers on the answer sheet.
5 Write clearly. You don't want to lose marks because the examiner can't read your writing!
6 When you do Part 1, make sure that you don't write more than three words for any answer.
7 When you do Part 2, remember to write something about each point in the instructions.
8 When you do Part 3, try to make your letter or story clear and interesting.
9 Near the end of the test time, check your answers.
10 There is more information about this paper in the **Get ready** boxes in this book. Make sure you read them again before the exam.

1 Speaking

1 How often do you do these things?

watch television	sometimes
go to the cinema	quite often
surf the Internet	not very often
go to a concert	occasionally
go to the theatre	very often
go clubbing	never

2 Match the things in this box with the different types of entertainment.

curtain	encore	website	commercial
interval	soap opera	programme	backing group
ticket	channel	soloist	chat room

3 Say what you like and dislike about each type of entertainment.

2 Vocabulary

1 Complete the text with words from the box. Use each word only once.

part	clap	reviews	rehearsal	screen	camera
performance	series	director	stage	studio	lines

An Actor speaks

As an actor, I much prefer working in the theatre to working on a film or a television (1) .... When I get a (2) .... in a play, I spend a long time learning my (3) .... and then there is a long period of (4) .... with the other actors before the first night. The good thing about a play, however, is that you are standing up on the (5) .... with a real live audience just a few metres away from you. At the end of the play, if they have enjoyed it, the people all (6) .... and you really feel good. It's interesting to read the (7) .... in the newspaper, but it's the people who are there who really matter. Working in film or television, however, you spend too much time waiting in the (8) .... while the (9) .... crew make all the technical arrangements. You sometimes have to do the same bit over and over again until the (10) .... is satisfied with your (11) .... Then it is months or even years before the film or programme appears on the (12) .... By then, you've forgotten all about it and you're in the middle of doing the next thing, anyway.

2 Choose the best answer, A, B, C, or D.

1 Why does the actor prefer working in the theatre?

A You have lots of time to practise.

B It's the same every night.

C There is a live audience.

D He always gets good reviews.

2 What does the actor dislike about working on films?
A It can be boring.
B You can get lonely.
C It is easy to forget your lines.
D You have to do two things at once.

3 Fill in the missing word in these sentences.

1 A .... is someone who writes in a magazine or newspaper.
2 A guitarist is someone who .... a guitar, often in a group.

4 Make similar sentences to explain what these people do.

drummer	director	photographer	TV presenter
disc jockey	comedian	pianist	film critic
interviewer	dancer	singer	violinist

3 Listening

1 Listen to two friends discussing what to do this evening. Where do they decide to go?

A ☐   B ☐   C ☐

2 Listen to two friends talking about films. Which type of film do they decide to go and see?

A ☐   B ☐   C ☐

3 Listen to two friends discussing a film they have each seen. What did they like most about the film?

A the plot
B the actors
C the camerawork

4 Speaking

Talk about a film, play or TV programme you have seen recently. Say what was good and bad about it. Remember to include information about the plot, camerawork and actors.

5 Listening

Get ready for PET Listening paper

1. You have about 30 minutes for the Listening paper.
2. There are four parts to the paper: Part 1 has seven short texts, and Parts 2, 3, and 4 have one long text each.
3. You can get 25 marks for the Listening paper, one for each question.
4. There are pauses between the listening texts. Make sure you use this time to read the questions for the next part, so you are ready to answer.
5. You hear each listening text twice. Answer the questions during the first listening. Check your answers when you hear the text for the second time.
6. In the exam you get a question paper and an answer sheet (see p.92-3). As you listen, write your answers on the question paper. At the end of the test, you have extra time to copy your answers on to the answer sheet.
7. You must use pencil on the answer sheet. Take a pencil, pencil sharpener and rubber to the exam.
8. Copy your answers carefully on to the answer sheet. Mark only one letter for each question. If you make a mistake, rub it out carefully and mark the new answer clearly.
9. Listen carefully, but don't worry if there are words you don't understand. You probably don't need to know them to answer the questions.
10. If there is a question you can't answer, just leave it and move on to the next one. You will probably hear the answer the second time you listen.
11. If you don't know the answer after the two listenings, guess – you may be right!
12. There is more information about this paper in the **Get ready** boxes in this book. Make sure you read them again before the exam.

Now try this listening task. Listen twice, as in the exam.

- Look at the notes about radio programmes.
- Some information is missing.
- You will hear an announcement about the programmes.
- For each question, fill in the missing information.

THIS MORNING'S RADIO

08.00	News
	Arts Review programme
(1)	– information about theatre, concerts and films
	– special guest: Kevin Jones, (2) .... in a pop band.
08.45	(3) .... with Graham Smith.
08.50	New series: Polly Brown talks to people about (4) ....
09.30	(5) .... with James Grant.
10.15	Radio play called (6) ' .... '

6 Writing

Your English teacher has asked you to write a story.
Your story must begin with this sentence:

When the taxi came, Sandra was ready in her best dress and shoes.

Write your story in about 100 words.

The age of communication

1 Speaking

1 Look at these ways of keeping in touch with people.

| letters | mobile phone | e-mail | fax | pager |

Talk about:
* how often you use each one
* what you use each one for
* the good and bad things about each one

2 Look at these two photographs. They both show people keeping in touch with their friends. Choose one of the photographs and talk about it. Remember to talk about all the things you can see, what the people are doing, and how you think they are feeling.

A

B

Get ready for PET Speaking paper

1 You have 10–12 minutes for the Speaking paper.

2 You take the test with another student who is your partner. There are two examiners: one tells you what to do and the other one listens. Remember to speak clearly so both examiners can hear you.

3 There are four parts to the paper: talking about yourself, a situation, a photograph, and discussing a wider theme.

4 You can get 25 marks for the Speaking paper. You get marks for how well you communicate with your partner and for your pronunciation. There are also some marks for grammar and vocabulary.

5 Listen carefully to the examiner's instructions. If you are not sure what to do, ask the examiner to repeat them.

6 In Parts 2 and 4, talk to your partner – not to the examiner.

7 In Parts 2 and 3 the pictures are there to help you. Talk about what you can see and don't stop after you have talked about one thing. If you can't remember the word for something, don't worry. You can describe the thing or talk about something else.

8 Try to make the test easier for your partner and the examiner by being relaxed and friendly. In Parts 2 and 4, remember to ask your partner questions, show an interest in what they say, and give them a chance to speak.

9 There is more information about this paper in the **Get ready** boxes in this book. Make sure you read them again before the exam.

3 **Practise this Part 2 task with a friend. Remember to talk about *all* the pictures, and don't decide too soon!**

The examiner says:

I'm going to describe a situation to you. A friend is going away to study in another town. She will be living on her own in a student flat. She has some money to spend on one piece of electrical equipment, but she doesn't know what to buy. Talk together about the different things she can buy, and then say which will be best.

4   **Remember, you will be asked to spell your name in Part 1 of the test. Practise spelling these words out loud in English:**

• your first name
• your family name

Read the text below and choose the correct word, A, B, C or D, for each space.

THE RECIPE FOR GOOD COMMUNICATION

How many people do you communicate with in a day? Probably a lot more **(1)** .... you did ten years ago. With a few pieces of equipment, we can 'talk' to people in more and more ways, not **(2)** .... face-to-face and on the phone, but also via the Internet. It is very important, therefore, **(3)** .... everyone to try and improve their communication skills. Despite all the technological advances of **(4)** .... years, the art of good conversation is still at the heart of successful communication. **(5)** .... it's a good idea to remember the four golden rules of good communication. Firstly, be as clear as you can. Misunderstandings arise if we don't say exactly **(6)** .... we mean. Secondly, we have to work **(7)** .... at listening. Pay attention to what the other person is saying. Thirdly, ask **(8)** .... people what they think, don't only tell them what you think. And finally show respect for people, give them time to say what they want, and **(9)** .... interest in what they say.
If you **(10)** .... these rules, you will be a good communicator.

1	**A** like	**B** than	**C** as	**D** that
2	**A** yet	**B** even	**C** just	**D** still
3	**A** for	**B** if	**C** by	**D** from
4	**A** close	**B** last	**C** late	**D** recent
5	**A** There	**B** So	**C** Such	**D** Or
6	**A** when	**B** what	**C** which	**D** whom
7	**A** hard	**B** much	**C** great	**D** very
8	**A** every	**B** other	**C** each	**D** another
9	**A** get	**B** put	**C** be	**D** show
10	**A** act	**B** move	**C** follow	**D** go

Complete the second sentence so that it means the same as the first, using no more than three words.

1   My parents prefer using the telephone to using e-mail.
    My parents think using the telephone is better .... e-mail.
2   My neighbour is confused by modern technology.
    Modern technology .... my neighbour.
3   Whose is this mobile phone?
    Who does this mobile phone .... to?
4   When I look at a screen for too long, I find it tiring.
    I get .... when I look at a screen for too long.
5   Why don't you send Anne a text message?
    If I were you, ... send Anne a text message.

PAPER 1   Reading and Writing Test   1 hour 30 minutes

READING

PART 1

Questions 1–5

- Look at the text in each question.
- What does it say?
- Mark the letter next to the correct explanation – **A**, **B** or **C** – on your answer sheet.

Example:

0

**These animals are
dangerous.
Do not cross the
safety fence.**

A Don't get any nearer to these animals
because they may hurt you.

B Don't let these animals get out from
behind this fence.

C It's dangerous to bring animals into this
area.

Example answer:

Part 1

0	A	B	C
	▬	☐	☐

1

**At night, check time of
last train before buying
ticket from this machine.**

A At night, you should get your train ticket
from this machine.

B Don't buy a ticket unless you're sure the
last train hasn't yet left.

C You needn't buy a ticket if you're travelling
on the last train.

2

*Bring your swimming things
tomorrow, although having a
swimming class depends on
the availability of the school
bus to take us to the pool.
Mr Davies*

A Students should come ready to have a
swimming class tomorrow.

B Students should catch the bus to the
swimming pool and meet Mr Davies there.

C Students should let Mr Davies know if they
aren't going to the swimming class.

3

CENTRAL HOSPITAL

**Mobile phones must be
switched off as they interrupt
the working of essential
medical equipment.**

A It's essential to switch off this equipment
before using your mobile phone.

B Don't use your mobile phone here
because it can prevent important
equipment from working.

C If this equipment doesn't work, use your
mobile phone to call for help.

4

E-mail:

To: Jaya
From: Gopal

I've booked our flight
and we pick up the
tickets at the airport.
If you think we need
insurance, can you see
about getting it?
            Gopal

What does Gopal want Jaya to do?

A arrange their journey to the airport

B meet him at the airport ticket desk

C be responsible for travel insurance

5

WARNING
*Heavy fines for leaving
rubbish inside Nature Park.
Use bins at gate.*

A You should close the gate behind you
when you leave the Nature Park.

B You can help us by picking up the rubbish
which has been left here.

C You'll have to pay if you don't put your
rubbish in the proper place.

TV PROGRAMMES TO ENJOY THIS EVENING

A Time to grow
Channel 1, 7.05 pm
Are we born or are we made? In the final part of this series following the development of 25 children born at the start of the 21st century, Dr Fiona Roberts looks at what happens when children don't get the training they need.

B Monkeys of the Rock
Channel 2, 7.15 pm
This programme visits the monkeys of Gibraltar, at the gateway to the Mediterranean sea. These animals are, in fact, Barbary macaques who, although they at times seem quite violent, have close and caring family relationships.

C City Hospital
Channel 4, 8.00 pm
Surprisingly, things are going smoothly for the characters in this popular series about life in a fictional hospital. Declan saves a child's life, Sara helps a young father to walk again, and Ant and Jo decide to go on holiday.

D Bird on the Wing
Channel 4, 9.00 pm
Comedy action thriller. Jack Rice is the last person his former girlfriend, Rachel, expects to meet in Chicago. When two criminals try to kill him, Rachel has to find out why these men and the police all want to know where Jack is. Will it end with tears or wedding bells?

E Help, I'm a Dentist
Channel 3, 9.00 pm
In this documentary, cameras follow five students from their first day in the classroom to the end of their first year's work as qualified dentists. We see what their studies involve and how the young dentists get on with each other, their teachers and their patients.

F Starship Police
Channel 5, 9.05 pm
Barker and his group of space officers discover a planet where the inhabitants have an unknown disease. But you'll have to wait until next week to see whether Truman, the ship's doctor, can find a cure before the space officers fall ill, too.

G Secret of the Bones
Channel 2, 9.10 pm
Have scientists uncovered what really happened 600 years ago high in the Andes mountains? This documentary shows how the bones of a young man found with a knife in his chest led Professor James Nolan to the killers.

H Ice Matters
Channel 1, 9.10 pm
The Arctic is one of the most beautiful places on earth, and also one of the hardest for living things. This programme looks at three different kinds of whale which manage to exist in its icy waters. They are the snow-white beluga, the 20-metre-long bowhead, and the narwhal.

PART 2

Questions 6–10

- The people below all want to watch something on television.
- On the opposite page, there are eight descriptions of television programmes.
- Decide which programme (letters **A–H**) would be the most suitable for each person (numbers **6–10**).
- For each of these numbers, mark the correct letter on your answer sheet.

6
Nadia watches television when she wants to relax. She'd like to see a drama where nothing violent happens and where everything ends well.

7
Laurence and his wife have just had their first baby and want a large family. He is keen to watch any documentary which will help him understand how to be a good father.

8
Olivia is wondering what to do when she leaves school. She may decide to become a doctor but she'd enjoy watching any programme which gives her factual information about a possible career.

9
Fabian is interested in all kinds of detective work. He likes thrillers but would always prefer to watch something about real-life crime.

10
Gwen is preparing a nature studies project for school about animals of the world's seas. She should watch any programme which will help her with this, rather than her favourite programme about space travel.

PRACTICE TEST 1 – READING

PART 3

Questions 11–20

- Look at the sentences below about acting in living history events.
- Read the text on the opposite page to decide if each sentence is correct or incorrect.
- If it is correct, mark **A** on your answer sheet.
- If it is not correct, mark **B** on your answer sheet.

11 During a living history event, children act the part of someone their age from the past.

12 Interest has grown in showing what happened in historic battles.

13 Howard Giles' organization is careful to present life in the past completely truthfully.

14 University professors find out useful information from watching living history events.

15 Young people have to work hard to benefit from being in a living history event.

16 Adults in the events spend all their time answering questions.

17 Katherine Goodman is confident about performing in public.

18 Katherine Goodman has learnt to trust what she reads in history books.

19 Owain Barry has grown bored with studying history.

20 Estelle Crump has a good opinion of everybody who was involved in the English Civil War.

Living history events

'Boy, bring me my gloves!' Immediately, seven-year-old Tim runs into the tent behind him. In seventeenth-century society, when an officer from the King's army gives you an order, it's best to be quick.

Tim is one of hundreds of children and adults taking part in living history events. This summer, while he acts out camp life during the English Civil War (1642–52), others like him will recreate the daily life of ordinary people from many different periods of history at numerous events across Britain.

Organizations which aim to recreate special events in history have existed for many years. However, until recently, these organizations concentrated mainly on famous battles. Nowadays, they have turned their attention to the everyday activities of ordinary people. Howard Giles, from the organization English Heritage, says: 'There is an increasing demand for our events and we put a lot of effort into making the details we show of life at the time exactly right.'

History professor Mick Aston of Bristol University says: 'Anything that helps people understand the past is valuable. Also, historians like me can learn from looking at the behaviour of the real people in these events. I'm interested in how they manage the small problems of everyday life.'

Whatever their age, young actors get a lot out of these historical events. They enjoy themselves and make new friends, but also learn a lot of history without even trying. This is because they spend hours watching their parents doing everyday jobs like cooking, shoemaking and carpentry in the manner of the period. They also listen while questions from members of the public watching the event are answered.

Katherine Goodman is only ten, but she has just spent nine days in a large old country house, acting out daily life there in 1587 for visiting schools. 'I never get embarrassed, even if someone laughs at me,' she says. According to Katherine, a lot of information about the period in schoolbooks is not to be believed. 'My teacher gets me to tell the other students when I notice something wrong.'

Taking part in events encourages young people to look at their classroom history lessons in a new light. 'I used to be bored by them,' says fifteen-year-old Owain Barry, who has been in many weekend events, 'but now I look forward to them.' Seventeen-year-old Estelle Crump, who has taken part since the age of eleven in English Civil War events, intends to study the period at university. 'The only problem is that at the moment I am firmly on one side in the war, but I'm going to have to learn to respect the point of view of the people on the other side as well!'

Copyright © Jerome Monahan, *The Guardian Education*, 18 July 2000.

PART 4

Questions 21–25

- Read the text and questions below.
- For each question, mark the letter next to the correct answer – **A, B, C** or **D** – on your answer sheet.

Young novelist
by Max Brady

Suzanne Todd has just won the Best New Writer prize for her first novel, *Roadrunner*. The idea for the book came from her own travels – four years ago she decided to give up her job in a bank to go round the world on her own for a year.

'I was tired of doing the same thing every day and wanted to find some excitement before it was too late,' she says. 'I felt so frightened sitting on the plane that I was counting the weeks until I could come back! But I saw many wonderful things, and in India I met Richard, who is now my husband.' Back home, she started writing *Roadrunner*. This novel is about Tara Roberts, who decides to give up her job and travel round the world, and it sounds like an autobiography. 'Tara goes to the same places as me and feels the same about them, but I don't have her wild way of behaving or attract danger as she does,' Suzanne explains.

Suzanne's second novel, called *Sailing*, shows Tara in different amusing situations and, unusually for second novels, is just as entertaining as the first. This is even more extraordinary when you consider that since the birth of her son, Suzanne has had to fit in time for writing around looking after him. 'I have to be better organized now,' she says. *Roadrunner* is going to be made into a film, a third and final novel about Tara is planned, and Suzanne is still only 29. How does she feel about her future? 'I just take things as they come,' she says with a smile.

21 What is Max Brady trying to do in this text?
   A review the first book written by a young novelist
   B explain what a writer had to do to win a prize
   C give some background information to the work of a writer
   D advise young people how to become successful writers

22 Why did Suzanne travel round the world?
   A She was sent by the newspaper she worked for.
   B She had arranged to meet her husband in India.
   C She wanted to cure her fear of flying.
   D She was keen to look for adventure.

23 Suzanne and the heroine of *Roadrunner*
   A have similar travel experiences.
   B have similar characters.
   C both write books about their journeys.
   D both lead dangerous lives.

24 How does Max Brady feel about *Sailing*?
   A He's disappointed Suzanne spent less time on it.
   B He's surprised Suzanne can repeat her success.
   C He's uninterested in reading more about the same person.
   D He's pleased she's included ideas about children in it.

25 Which of these can you read on the cover of *Sailing*?

A
Suzanne Todd is married with one child. This, her second novel, has been made into a film starring Tara Roberts.

B
Suzanne Todd went on a trip around the world four years ago and this is the travel book she wrote about her journey.

C
Suzanne Todd has gone from being a bank clerk to a prize-winning writer. This novel is second in a series of three.

D
Suzanne Todd is not yet 30, but has already completed three novels. This one continues the story of Tara and will make you laugh aloud.

PART 5

Questions 26–35

- Read the text below and choose the correct word for each space.
- For each question, mark the letter next to the correct word – **A, B, C** or **D** – on your answer sheet.

Example answer:

Part 5
0   A   B   C   D

CROSSING A LAND OF ICE

Pollyanna Murray and Natasha Wight have **(0)** ...... the first women to cross Bylot, an island of ice and snow-covered mountains in the Arctic Circle. The journey began in Greenland, from where they **(26)** ...... off for Bylot in a small sailing boat. 'We nearly **(27)** ...... an iceberg and that would have done serious **(28)** ...... to our boat!' says Pollyanna. When the women finally got to the 100-kilometre-long island, all they **(29)** ...... see were the marks made in the snow by polar bears. 'We slept with a gun beside us because we were afraid **(30)** ...... might attack us.' **(31)** ...... the walk across the island, the women had to **(32)** ...... their food on their backs and soon they didn't have **(33)** ...... left. 'Walking eleven hours a day with just chocolate to eat made us very **(34)** ...... ,' says Pollyanna. But after seven days, the pair **(35)** ...... the other side of the island safely.

		A		B		C		D	
0		become		appeared		succeeded		done	
26	A	called	B	set	C	passed	D	pulled
27	A	crashed	B	ran	C	hit	D	slipped
28	A	damage	B	breakdown	C	fault	D	ruin
29	A	should	B	did	C	have	D	could
30	A	all	B	it	C	he	D	one
31	A	For	B	By	C	Through	D	Along
32	A	hold	B	contain	C	carry	D	deliver
33	A	some	B	much	C	many	D	everything
34	A	dull	B	weak	C	poor	D	soft
35	A	arrived	B	came	C	reached	D	entered

WRITING

PART 1

Questions 1–5

- Here are some sentences about learning to drive.
- For each question, finish the second sentence so that it means the same as the first, **using no more than three words.**
- Write only the missing words on your answer sheet.
- You may use this page for any rough work.

Example: My father agreed to pay for my driving lessons.

My father said, 'Yes, I *will pay* for your driving lessons.'

1 At first, I didn't find it easy to drive.

At first, I .... it difficult to drive.

2 'Follow my instructions and you'll be a good driver,' said my teacher.

'Follow my instructions and you'll drive ....,' said my teacher.

3 My driving teacher is more patient than my friend's teacher.

My friend's driving teacher isn't .... mine.

4 When I'm more confident about overtaking, I can take my driving test.

I can't take my driving test .... I'm more confident about overtaking.

5 When I have my driving licence, I'll borrow my father's car.

When I have my driving licence, my father will .... his car.

PART 2

Question 6

You spent yesterday evening in the house of your English friend, Chris. Write a card to Chris. In your card, you should

- thank Chris
- say what you particularly enjoyed about the evening
- invite Chris to do something with you

Write **35–45 words** on your answer sheet.

PART 3

Answer **one** of the following questions (**7 or 8**).
Write about **100 words** on your answer sheet.

Question 7

• This is part of a letter you receive from your English penfriend.

*I play the guitar and sing in a rock band. We sometimes
play at our friends' parties. Tell me about the music you
like listening to. Can you play a musical instrument?*

• Now write a letter to your penfriend about the music you like.
• Write your **letter** in about **100 words** on your answer sheet.

Question 8

• Your English teacher has asked you to write a story.
• This is the title for your story:

The new shoes

• Write your **story** in about **100 words** on your answer sheet.

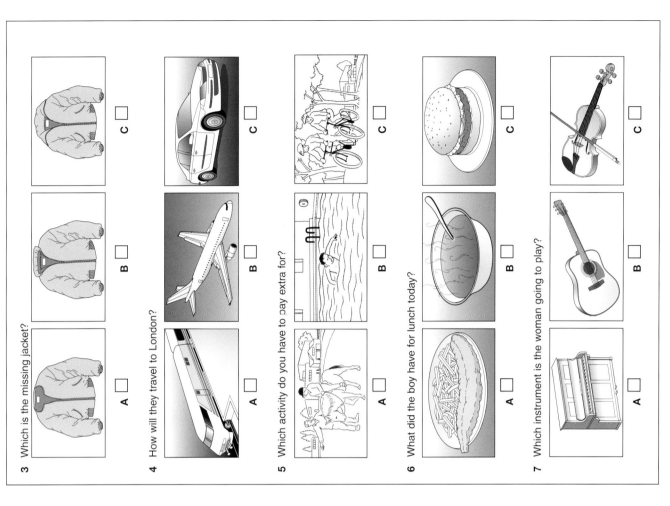

3 Which is the missing jacket?

A ☐   B ☐   C ☐

4 How will they travel to London?

A ☐   B ☐   C ☐

5 Which activity do you have to pay extra for?

A ☐   B ☐   C ☐

6 What did the boy have for lunch today?

A ☐   B ☐   C ☐

7 Which instrument is the woman going to play?

A ☐   B ☐   C ☐

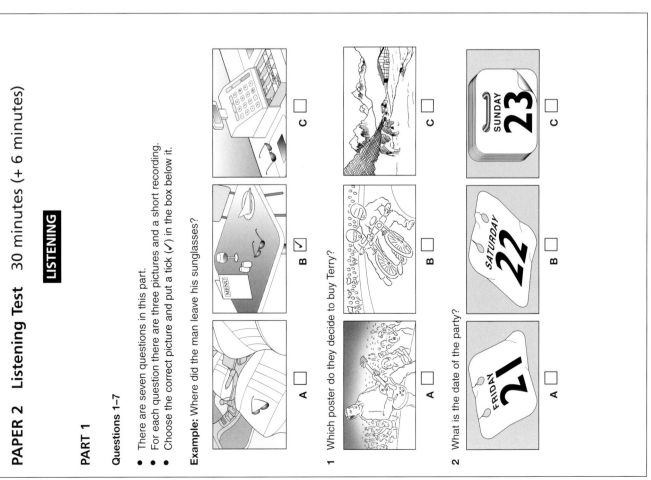

PAPER 2   Listening Test   30 minutes (+ 6 minutes)

LISTENING

PART 1

Questions 1–7

- There are seven questions in this part.
- For each question there are three pictures and a short recording.
- Choose the correct picture and put a tick (✓) in the box below it.

Example: Where did the man leave his sunglasses?

A ☐   B ☑   C ☐

1 Which poster do they decide to buy Terry?

A ☐   B ☐   C ☐

2 What is the date of the party?

A ☐   B ☐   C ☐

PART 2

Questions 8–13

- You will hear an interview with a young artist called Mauro Matthews.
- For each question, put a tick (✔) in the correct box.

8 When he was a child, Mauro
   wanted to work in

   A ☐ a hotel.
   B ☐ an art gallery.
   C ☐ the army.

9 What subject did Mauro enjoy
   most at school?

   A ☐ music
   B ☐ languages
   C ☐ mathematics

10 Why did Mauro go to
   Florence?

   A ☐ to learn how to paint
   B ☐ to improve his Italian
   C ☐ to find out about art history

11 Why did Mauro leave
   university?

   A ☐ He argued with the other students.
   B ☐ He found the course too difficult for him.
   C ☐ He wasn't doing the type of painting he liked.

12 How does Mauro make
   enough money to live?

   A ☐ by working in an art gallery
   B ☐ by selling some of his paintings
   C ☐ by doing paintings of famous people

13 Mauro says that young artists
   should

   A ☐ do what other artists are doing.
   B ☐ follow the advice of experts.
   C ☐ believe in their own ideas.

PART 3

Questions 14–19

- You will hear a woman giving a talk about holidays in the Caribbean.
- For each question, fill in the missing information in the numbered space.

HOLIDAYS IN THE CARIBBEAN

Later in the talk, people can see (14) .... of the Caribbean.

The price of holidays usually includes food, drink and (15) ....

In Jamaica, some holidays cost up to (16) £ ....

The rainy season generally starts in the month of (17) ....

The best foreign currency to use in the area is (18) ....

In Cuba, visitors must pay for a (19) .... when they arrive.

PART 4

Questions 20–25

- Look at the six sentences for this part.
- You will hear a conversation between a girl, Olga, and a boy, Marc.
- Decide if each sentence is correct or incorrect.
- If it is correct, put a tick (✓) in the box under **A** for **YES**. If it is not correct, put a tick (✓) in the box under **B** for **NO**.

		A YES	B NO
20	Olga thanks Marc for buying the concert tickets.	☐	☐
21	Olga agrees that her mother is being unreasonable.	☐	☐
22	Olga is surprised at the price of the tickets.	☐	☐
23	Marc is happy to go to the concert alone.	☐	☐
24	Olga suggests someone who would enjoy the concert.	☐	☐
25	Olga refuses to suggest a new plan to her mother.	☐	☐

PRACTICE TEST 1 – SPEAKING

PAPER 3 Speaking Test about 12 minutes

PART 1 (2–3 minutes)

The test begins with a general conversation with the examiner, who will ask you and the other candidate some questions about yourselves. Be ready to talk about your daily life, your studies, your likes and dislikes, etc. In this part, you will be asked to spell all or part of your name.

PART 2 (2–3 minutes)

The examiner says:

In the next part, you will talk to each other. I'm going to describe a situation to you. Your English teacher is leaving the school to go and work in another country. You would like to buy her a present. Talk together about the types of present you could buy, and then decide which would be best.

See example visual on p. 77.

PART 3 (3 minutes)

The examiner says:

Now I'd like each of you to talk on your own about something. I'm going to give each of you a photograph of people doing things at home. Please tell us what you can see in your photograph.

See example photographs on p. 78.

PART 4 (3 minutes)

The examiner says:

*Your photographs showed people doing things at home. Now I'd like you to talk about things you **have** to do at home, and the things you **enjoy** doing at home.*

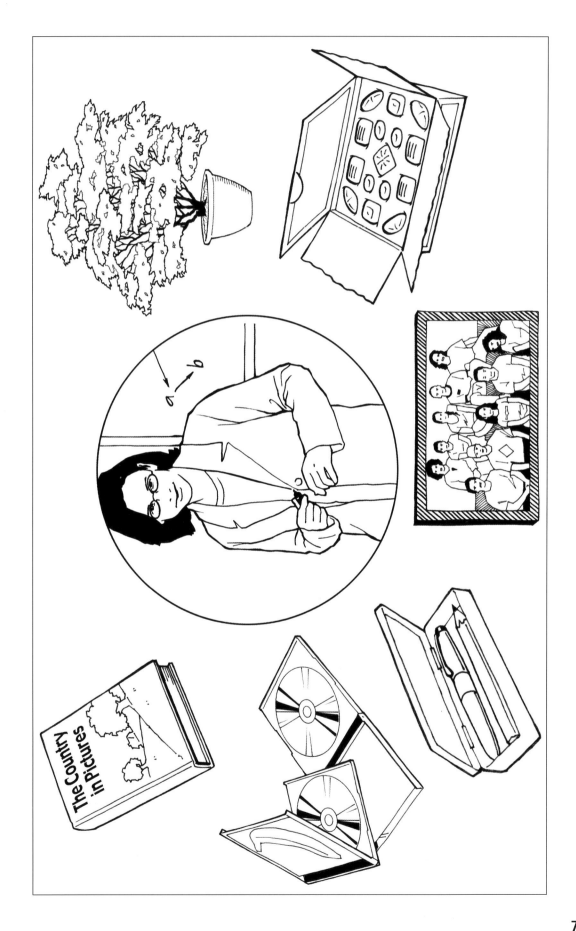

PAPER 1 Reading and Writing Test 1 hour 30 minutes

READING

PART 1

Questions 1–5

- Look at the text in each question.
- What does it say?
- Mark the letter next to the correct explanation – **A**, **B** or **C** – on your answer sheet.

Example:

0

> **These animals are dangerous.**
> **Do not cross the safety fence.**

A Don't get any nearer to these animals because they may hurt you.

B Don't let these animals get out from behind this fence.

C It's dangerous to bring animals into this area.

Example answer:

Part 1

0	A	B	C
	■		

1

> **E-mail:**
> **To:** Barnet Hotel
> **From:** James Mead
> **Re:** Booking change
>
> Can we include a child's bed in the double room we've booked for 3 nights from 2 January? Thanks.

James Mead wants to book a room

A on a different date.

B for more people.

C for a longer time.

2

> Anyone behaving badly and disturbing other swimmers will be asked to leave the pool.

A You'll have to leave the pool if you annoy other swimmers.

B You are only permitted to use this pool if you can swim well.

C You can ask for help here if you'd like to improve your swimming.

3

> **message**
>
> Emma,
> Your tennis coach says you can't play in the under-16s competition tomorrow unless you show your birth certificate when you register. So don't forget it!
> Mum

A According to her tennis coach, Emma isn't old enough to play in tomorrow's competition.

B Emma can't play tomorrow because she forgot to register for the competition.

C If Emma leaves her birth certificate behind tomorrow, she won't be allowed to play.

4

> **Great value electronic goods!**
> **Money back if not satisfied.**
> **Receipts must be produced.**

A We give money back on old electronic goods when you buy new ones here.

B Bring your receipt with you next time to buy goods at a cheaper price.

C We will return your money if you show a receipt for what you've bought.

5

> P O S T
>
> Dear Tim,
> Olga and I should have met at the top of this tower, but she went shopping instead without telling me! Never mind, I enjoyed the view on my own.
> See you soon,
> Tom

A Tom accompanied Olga on a shopping trip.

B Olga didn't meet Tom as they had planned.

C Tom and Olga climbed a tower together.

PRACTICE TEST 2 – READING

PART 2

Questions 6–10

- The people below all want to go on a weekend course.
- On the opposite page, there are eight descriptions of weekend courses.
- Decide which course (letters **A–H**) would be the most suitable for each person (numbers **6–10**).
- For each of these numbers, mark the correct letter on your answer sheet.

6

Carl's garden is in a terrible state. He would like to make it look nice, but as he's never done this kind of work before, he doesn't know where to start.

7

Lily has tried to paint using both watercolours and oils, but without success. She'd now like to experiment with using her camera instead to create beautiful pictures.

8

Whitney already knows a lot about modern art, but now she'd like to learn something about artists working in the fourteenth and fifteenth centuries.

9

Bruno is interested in biology and wants to find out about all the living things in his neighbourhood. He prefers to make discoveries for himself rather than listen to lectures.

10

Sylvia is planning a trip around the world to look at wildlife. She thinks she'll enjoy it more if she learns a bit about some of the wild things she may see before she leaves.

Weekend courses at The Countryside College

A Personal view

On this exciting course, we show students how to take artistic photographs using simple methods. Recording memorable images, ideas and feelings depends more on being able to 'see' your picture before you take it than on owning expensive equipment.

B Understanding the modern

By the end of the nineteenth century, artists were producing pictures which, to traditional taste, seemed shocking and laughable. Making use of slides and photographs, we shall look at the ideas behind this art and see how they led to the art movements of the twentieth and twenty-first centuries.

C Hidden world

Following instructions from the teacher, students will see what forms of insect life they can find in the college gardens, and what they can learn about them. We will also help you put together some simple equipment so you can continue on your own to watch, photograph and collect many different kinds of insect.

D Watercolour art

This course in painting the countryside in watercolours will give beginners the confidence to make skilful pictures of skies, trees, water and buildings. There will be opportunities to paint outdoors in the beautiful college gardens and to take quick photos which can be turned into paintings later.

E Japanese gardens

We will discuss how to design and make Japanese gardens. Students will then go on to study how to create miniature trees (bonsai). The course begins with demonstrations, followed by practical work by students, who should already have some experience of gardening.

F Great masters

In this course, the work of masters such as Jan Van Eyck (died 1441) and Donatello (1386–1466) is studied. Students will look at how Van Eyck used the newly-invented oil paint to create wonderful pictures, and at how Donatello brought great feeling to sculpture in marble, stone and wood.

G Green fingers

Whether you are starting with a bare piece of earth, or need to bring a fresh look to an existing garden, this course can help. Using lectures and practical work, we'll give you the basic rules of garden design together with many ideas for you to try out back home.

H Sight and sound

Recognizing birds, even unfamiliar ones, becomes easy when you know how. Photographs, slides and video, and sound recordings will accompany the lectures. This course is aimed at those who want to take their interest beyond the garden and students will learn the skills needed to identify birds from all continents.

Whale-watching in Newfoundland, Canada

Sarah Tucker goes eye to eye with the world's largest animals

I was swimming in cold, dark water and looking straight into the eye of a whale. The whale was less than 100 metres away and seemed as large as a cathedral. All I could hear was the sound of my heart beating. It was the experience of a lifetime.

● The Newfoundland coast

I went whale-watching in Bay Bulls, about 50 kilometres south of St John's, which is the capital of the island of Newfoundland, the most easterly point of North America. Bay Bulls is no further north than Paris is, but feels much colder thanks to the winds which blow in from the Arctic. Twenty-two different kinds of whale swim through the rich feeding waters along the island's coast, making Newfoundland one of the best places in the world to look for these huge creatures. This means that in Bay Bulls you can expect to see greater numbers of whales than sightseeing boats. I sailed with Wildland Tours and my guide was the naturalist, David Snow. Wildland Tours always makes sure you're accompanied by a local expert like him so you don't miss anything the island has to offer.

● A memorable experience

As we got in our boat, David said, 'Whales are very gentle and curious animals. They like to have a good look at us but if we're not in their way, they don't worry about us.' So as not to stress the whales or other wildlife, Wildland Tours limits the size of its tourist groups and only uses small boats. We watched for signs of whales and then headed towards them. David can recognize the type of whale even from a great distance. 'They're minke,' he said, pointing to a spot on the horizon. I asked him if they'd get close enough for me to reach out and feel their skin. 'It has been known, but I wouldn't recommend you to try it,' he said. David showed me how to dive into the water, warning me to stay close to our boat. And then it happened. A huge shadow of blue-black turned and a great mountain lifted from the sea, looked straight at me, and then fell beneath the waves again. David told me the whale looked at me for just a second, but it seemed an age.

● Further details

For more information about having an experience like mine, visit the Wildland Tours website (www.wildlands.com). While the company can't promise that you'll see whales, they've had 100 per cent viewing success in the last few years. In addition, on some tours there's the opportunity to take part in scientific research into the habits of these fascinating animals.

PART 3

Questions 11–20

- Look at the sentences below about a whale-watching trip.
- Read the text on the opposite page to decide if each sentence is correct or incorrect.
- If it is correct, mark **A** on your answer sheet.
- If it is not correct, mark **B** on your answer sheet.

11 The capital of Newfoundland is south of Bay Bulls.

12 Bay Bulls has the same kind of weather as Paris.

13 Newfoundland is good for whale-watching because whales can find a lot of food there.

14 In Bay Bulls, there are often fewer whales than tour boats in the water.

15 Guides working for Wildland Tours know a lot about their subject and come from the area.

16 Whales become anxious when people approach them in small boats.

17 It's difficult for David Snow to name different types of whale until they come near.

18 David advises tourists against touching the whales.

19 On a Wildlands Tours trip, tourists are likely to find what they've gone to see.

20 Some tourists are able to help scientists find out more about how whales behave.

PART 4

Questions 21–25

- Read the text and questions below.
- For each question, mark the letter next to the correct answer – **A**, **B**, **C** or **D** – on your answer sheet.

Stars for a day

Television programmes where ordinary people sing in competition against each other have become very popular. This is probably because everyone believes that, given the chance, they could be pop stars! Brian Tuitt, ex-drummer with Bad Manners and owner of Backline Studios, has noticed this. He provides people with half a day in the studio with a sound engineer, during which they make a CD singing their favourite song. Tuitt welcomes anyone of any age or musical ability to his studios. The service costs £125 per session, which includes one copy of the CD.

I took my daughter and five friends to Backline Studios as a twelfth birthday present. Six is the maximum number that can sensibly take part in the four-hour session. Fewer would have more time to try and improve their performances, but they would probably have less fun. The girls chose to sing Britney's 'Oops! I did it again'. Three, including my daughter, were confident enough to sing on their own and had each chosen a different part of the song, while the others preferred a backing role.

The girls were excited but nervous, and fortunately the sound engineer, Alistair Cowan, ex-singer with rock band Redwood, knew how to make them relax. He put them in a small recording studio where they sang their parts two at a time and where nobody could watch them. Cowan did all the technical work on the girls' recording and also all the artwork for the CD cover. He then sent them into a larger room to dance to their recording while I videoed them. The girls loved the whole experience and the CD is a valued souvenir.

Adapted from an article from *Time Out London* June 26–July 3 2002, entitled 'Idol Pleasures' by Sara O'Reilly. Reproduced by kind permission of Time Out Group ©.

21 What is the writer's main purpose in writing the text?

- **A** to encourage young people to take up a singing career
- **B** to inform people dreaming of being singers of a service
- **C** to describe what happens in different recording studios
- **D** to suggest ways parents can make their children feel confident

22 For £125, Brian Tuitt will

- **A** train people to sing in competitions on television.
- **B** give people advice about pop songs they've written.
- **C** let people watch a pop star recording a CD.
- **D** let people use his studios' facilities for a few hours.

23 The writer recommends taking a group of six to Backline because

- **A** a bigger group would cost too much money.
- **B** a bigger group wouldn't find a suitable song.
- **C** a smaller group wouldn't perform so well.
- **D** a smaller group wouldn't find it so enjoyable.

24 When the writer's daughter and her friends made their CD, they

- **A** recorded their voices in pairs.
- **B** sang and danced at the same time.
- **C** copied what they saw on a video.
- **D** performed in front of all the studio staff.

25 Which of these could be the writer's daughter speaking?

A My mum and I had a great time at Backline Studios. We sang Britney's song 'Oops! I did it again' together.

B My best birthday present was making a CD at Backline Studios. The picture on the cover is something I drew.

C My friends and I performed like real pop stars at Backline Studios. You can hear me singing by myself in one part of this CD.

D The people at Backline Studios were brilliant. They seem to know how singers feel, even though they've never performed themselves.

PART 5

Questions 26–35

- Read the text below and choose the correct word for each space.
- For each question, mark the letter next to the correct word – **A**, **B**, **C** or **D** – on your answer sheet.

Example answer:

Part 5
0	A	B	C	D
	■			

MEMORIES OF SCHOOL

My clearest memory of school is that it was **(0)** ...... fun. I've always **(26)** ...... on well with people and I loved it from the start. On my first day, **(27)** ...... was my mum who was crying at the school gates, while I ran happily inside. I was quite bright and often finished my schoolwork early, which left **(28)** ...... of time for chatting! All my teachers **(29)** ...... to say to my mum, 'Your daughter would do better if she talked less.' The maths teacher, Mr Earl, **(30)** ...... sticks in my mind. I was hopeless **(31)** ...... maths and I still can't add up, but Mr Earl realized that I had other skills and always **(32)** ...... my acting ability. On my **(33)** ...... day at school, he showed me an advertisement for an acting **(34)** ...... at a local theatre. Luckily, they **(35)** ...... someone just like me and I've been a professional actor ever since.

0	**A** great	**B** big	**C** large	**D** full
26	**A** gone	**B** she	**C** kept	**D** held
27	**A** she	**B** there	**C** it	**D** one
28	**A** plenty	**B** lot	**C** enough	**D** much
29	**A** did	**B** could	**C** ought	**D** used
30	**A** extremely	**B** singly	**C** exactly	**D** particularly
31	**A** by	**B** on	**C** at	**D** for
32	**A** encouraged	**B** suggested	**C** insured	**D** offered
33	**A** latest	**B** final	**C** closing	**D** finished
34	**A** work	**B** employment	**C** job	**D** occupation
35	**A** missed	**B** needed	**C** wished	**D** asked

83

PRACTICE TEST 2 – WRITING

WRITING

PART 1

Questions 1–5

- Here are some sentences about postage stamps.
- For each question, finish the second sentence so that it means the same as the first, **using no more than three words.**
- Write only the missing words on your answer sheet.
- You may use this page for any rough work.

Example: Postage stamps weren't used on letters until 1840.
People *didn't* use postage stamps on letters until 1840.

1 There was a picture of Queen Victoria on the first British stamp.
The first British stamp .... a picture of Queen Victoria on it.

2 People began collecting stamps at that time.
People .... stamps since that time.

3 Stamp-collecting can be quite a cheap hobby.
Stamp-collecting needn't be .... hobby.

4 For information about a country's history, look at its stamps.
If you want to .... about a country's history, look at its stamps.

5 There isn't a stamp in the world more valuable than the *British Guiana one-cent magenta.*
The world's .... stamp is the *British Guiana one-cent magenta.*

PART 2

Question 6

You have started studying a new subject.
Write an e-mail to your English friend, Robin. In your e-mail, you should

- tell Robin what you're studying
- describe the teacher
- say how you feel about the subject

Write **35–45 words** on your answer sheet.

PART 3

Answer **one** of the following questions (**7 or 8**).
Write about **100 words** on your answer sheet.

Question 7
- This is part of a letter you receive from some English friends.

> *Here are some photos of our wedding. We're sorry you couldn't be there. Have you been to a wedding recently? How do you celebrate weddings in your country?*

- Now write a letter to these friends about weddings in your country.
- Write your **letter** in about **100 words** on your answer sheet.

Question 8
- Your English teacher has asked you to write a story.
- Your story must begin with this sentence:

  Harry often went to the beach although he couldn't swim.

- Write your **story** in about **100 words** on your answer sheet.

PRACTICE TEST 2 – LISTENING

PAPER 2   Listening Test   30 minutes (+ 6 minutes)

LISTENING

PART 1

Questions 1–7

- There are seven questions in this part.
- For each question there are three pictures and a short recording.
- Choose the correct picture and put a tick (✓) in the box below it.

Example: Where did the man leave his sunglasses?

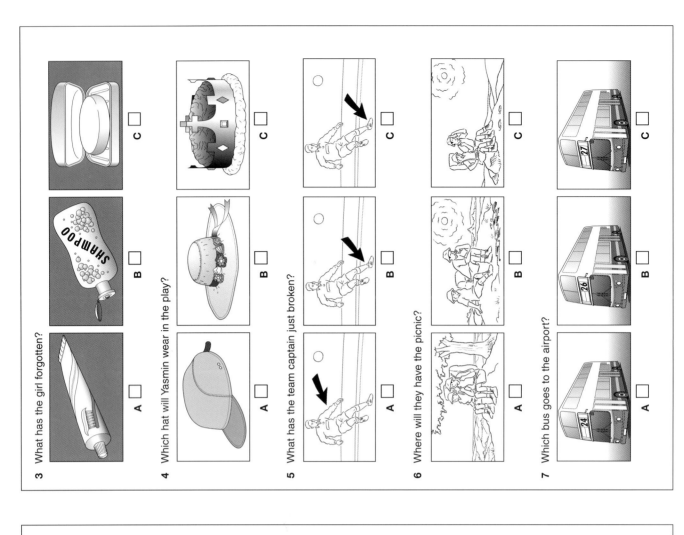

A ☐   B ☑   C ☐

1   What time does the film begin?

A ☐   B ☐   C ☐

2   What does the man want to borrow?

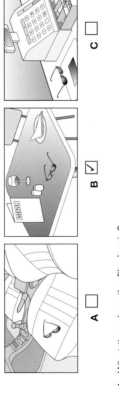

A ☐   B ☐   C ☐

3   What has the girl forgotten?

A ☐   B ☐   C ☐

4   Which hat will Yasmin wear in the play?

A ☐   B ☐   C ☐

5   What has the team captain just broken?

A ☐   B ☐   C ☐

6   Where will they have the picnic?

A ☐   B ☐   C ☐

7   Which bus goes to the airport?

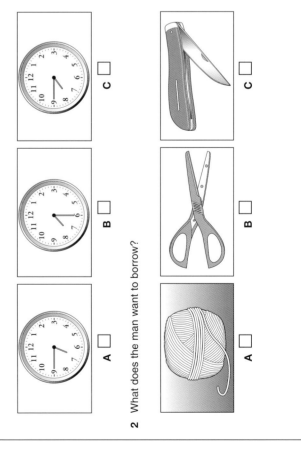

A ☐   B ☐   C ☐

PART 2

Questions 8–13

- You will hear part of a radio programme about a holiday in Italy where you learn how to cook.
- For each question, put a tick (✓) in the correct box.

8   How did Adrian first hear about the holiday?

   A ☐ from a friend
   B ☐ on a television programme
   C ☐ in a newspaper advertisement

9   What surprised Adrian about the island?

   A ☐ how good the beaches were
   B ☐ how few tourists were there
   C ☐ how interesting the ancient ruins were

10 What does Adrian say about the cooking lessons?

   A ☐ They were very difficult.
   B ☐ The teacher was very good.
   C ☐ It was like being at school.

11 The pizza which Adrian made

   A ☐ didn't look right.
   B ☐ didn't taste very nice.
   C ☐ wasn't properly cooked.

12 What disappointed Adrian about the holiday?

   A ☐ He sometimes felt lonely.
   B ☐ The other people were unfriendly.
   C ☐ He was the only young person there.

13 What is Adrian planning to do?

   A ☐ cook Italian food for his friends
   B ☐ take his friends to Italy next year
   C ☐ go on a different cooking holiday

PART 3

Questions 14–19

- You will hear a radio announcement about a film club.
- For each question, fill in the missing information in the numbered space.

THE VALLEY FILM CLUB

JOINING THE CLUB

Annual fee for members: **(14)** £ ....

                        (20% student discount)

WEEKLY FILM PROGRAMME

   Tuesdays: European films (with subtitles)

   Thursdays: **(15)** ....

   Saturdays: Romantic comedies

THIS YEAR'S FILM FESTIVAL

Month of Film Festival: **(16)** ....

Topic of the Film Festival: **(17)** ....

SPECIAL EVENTS

   November: **(18)** .... for one week

   August: **(19)** .... for one week

PRACTICE TEST 2 – LISTENING

PART 4

Questions 20–25

- Look at the six sentences for this part.
- You will hear a conversation between a girl, Lucy, and a boy, Tony.
- Decide if each sentence is correct or incorrect.
- If it is correct, put a tick (✓) in the box under **A** for **YES**. If it is not correct, put a tick (✓) in the box under **B** for **NO**.

	A YES	B NO
20 Tony is surprised that Lucy knows about his new motorbike.	☐	☐
21 Tony still needs to save the money for his ticket to Canada.	☐	☐
22 Tony is buying the motorbike from his cousin.	☐	☐
23 Lucy thinks that Tony's family is more generous than hers.	☐	☐
24 Lucy has ridden a large motorbike before.	☐	☐
25 Tony promises to let Lucy ride on his new motorbike.	☐	☐

PAPER 3 Speaking Test about 12 minutes

PART 1 (2–3 minutes)

The test begins with a general conversation with the examiner, who will ask you and the other candidate some questions about yourselves. Be ready to talk about your daily life, your studies, your likes and dislikes, etc. In this part, you will be asked to spell all or part of your name.

PART 2 (2–3 minutes)

The examiner says:

IIn the next part, you will talk to each other. I'm going to describe a situation to you. A young family from abroad is coming on holiday to this country. They have very little money, but want to see as much as possible. Talk together about the different ways of travelling around the country and say which will be best for them.

See example visual on p. 90.

PART 3 (3 minutes)

The examiner says:

Now I'd like each of you to talk on your own about something. I'm going to give each of you a photograph of people and animals. Tell us what you can see in your photograph.

See example photographs on p. 91.

PART 4 (3 minutes)

The examiner says:

*Your photographs showed people and animals. Now I'd like you to talk about the kind of animals which are **good** to keep as pets, and the kind of animals which are **not so good** as pets.*

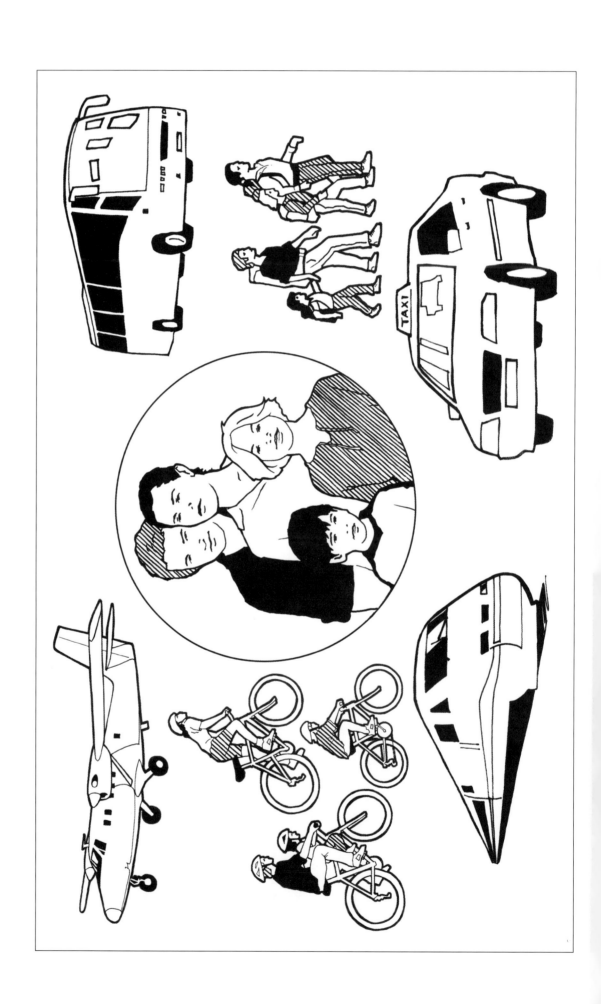

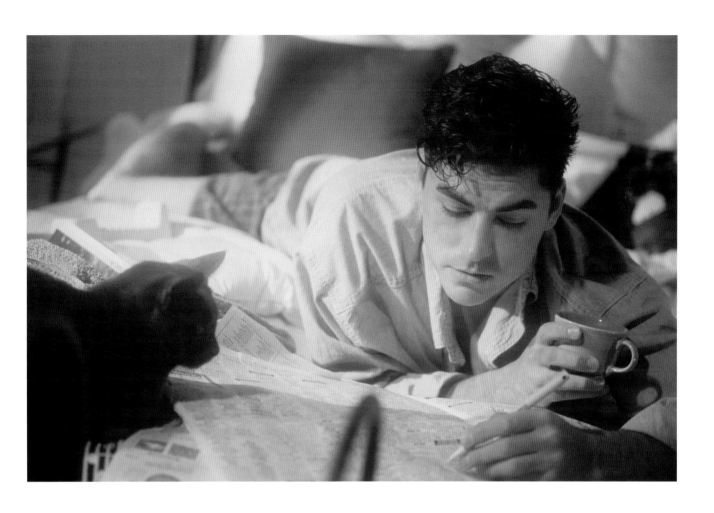

ANSWER SHEETS

READING AND WRITING – ANSWER SHEET 1

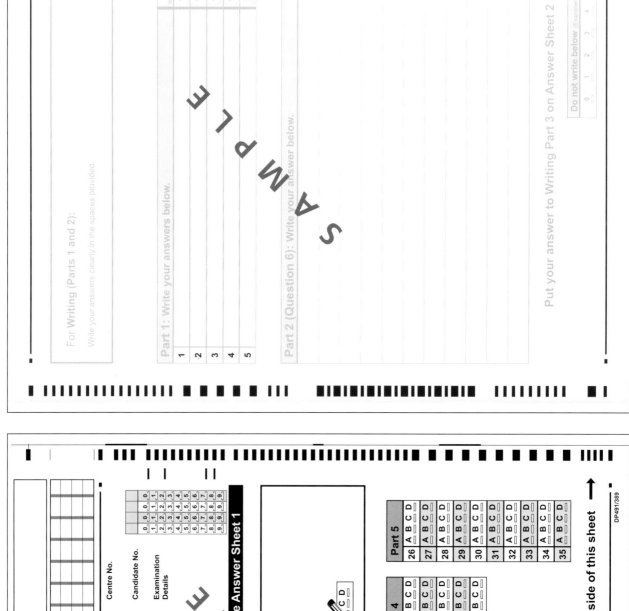

UNIVERSITY *of* CAMBRIDGE
ESOL Examinations

Candidate Name
If not already printed, write name
in CAPITALS and complete the
Candidate No. grid (in pencil).

Candidate Signature

Examination Title

Centre

Supervisor:

If the candidate is ABSENT or has WITHDRAWN shade here ☐

Centre No.

Candidate No.

Examination
Details

PET Paper 1 Reading and Writing Candidate Answer Sheet 1

Instructions

Use a **PENCIL** (B or HB).

Rub out any answer you want to change with an eraser.

For **Reading**:
Mark ONE letter for each question.
For example, if you think **A** is the right answer to the
question, mark your answer sheet like this:

0 | A̲ C D

Part 1	
1	A B C
2	A B C
3	A B C
4	A B C
5	A B C

Part 2	
6	A B C D E F G H
7	A B C D E F G H
8	A B C D E F G H
9	A B C D E F G H
10	A B C D E F G H

Part 3	
11	A B
12	A B
13	A B
14	A B
15	A B
16	A B
17	A B
18	A B
19	A B
20	A B

Part 4	
21	A B C D
22	A B C D
23	A B C D
24	A B C D
25	A B C D

Part 5	
26	A B C D
27	A B C D
28	A B C D
29	A B C D
30	A B C D
31	A B C D
32	A B C D
33	A B C D
34	A B C D
35	A B C D

Continue on the other side of this sheet →

PET RW 1

DP491/389

© UCLES

READING AND WRITING – ANSWER SHEET 1 (REVERSE)

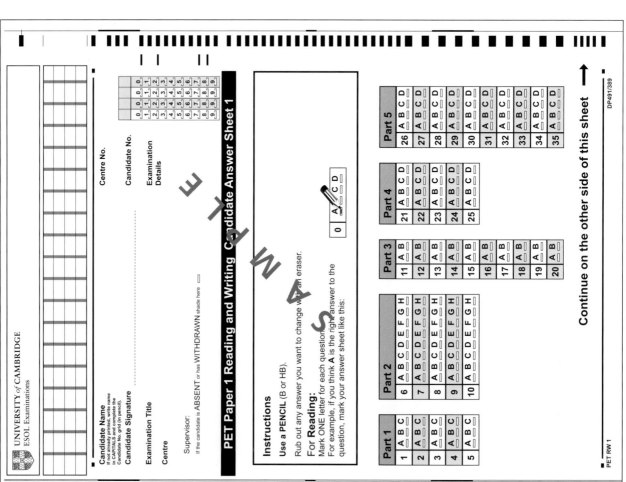

For Writing (Parts 1 and 2):

Write your answers clearly in the spaces provided

Part 1: Write your answers below.

1
2
3
4
5

Part 2 (Question 6): Write your answer below.

Put your answer to Writing Part 3 on Answer Sheet 2 →

Do not write below (Examiner use only)

© UCLES

LISTENING – ANSWER SHEET

UNIVERSITY of CAMBRIDGE
ESOL Examinations

Candidate Name
If not already printed, write name in CAPITALS and complete the Candidate No. grid (in pencil).

Candidate Signature

Examination Title

Centre

Supervisor:
If the candidate is ABSENT or has WITHDRAWN shade here ☐

Centre No.

Candidate No.

Examination Details

PET Paper 2 Listening Candidate Answer Sheet

You must transfer all your answers from the Listening Question Paper to this answer sheet.

Instructions

Use a PENCIL (B or HB).

Rub out any answer you want to change with an eraser.

For **Parts 1, 2** and **4**:
Mark ONE letter for each question.
For example, if you think **A** is the right answer to the question, mark your answer sheet like this:

0 ☐A☐ ☐C☐

For **Part 3**:
Write your answers clearly in the spaces next to the numbers (14 to 19) like this:

0 | example

Part 1			
1	A	B	C
2	A	B	C
3	A	B	C
4	A	B	C
5	A	B	C
6	A	B	C
7	A	B	C

Part 2			
8	A	B	C
9	A	B	C
10	A	B	C
11	A	B	C
12	A	B	C
13	A	B	C

Part 3	
14	
15	
16	
17	
18	
19	

Do not write here
1 14 0
1 15 0
1 16 0
1 17 0
1 18 0
1 19 0

Part 4		
20	A	B
21	A	B
22	A	B
23	A	B
24	A	B
25	A	B

PET L

DP493/391

© **UCLES**

READING AND WRITING – ANSWER SHEET 2

Part 3: Mark the number of the question you are answering here ➡ Q7 ☐ or Q8 ☐
Write your answer below.

Do not write below this line

This section for use by SECOND Examiner only

Mark:

0	1.1	1.2	1.3	2.1	2.2	2.3	3.1	3.2	3.3	4.1	4.2	4.3	5.1	5.2	5.3

Examiner Number:

0	1	2	3	4	5	6	7	8	9
0	1	2	3	4	5	6	7	8	9
0	1	2	3	4	5	6	7	8	9

© **UCLES**

93

Irregular verbs

present	past simple	past participle	present	past simple	past participle
be	was/were	been	learn	learnt	learnt
beat	beat	beaten	leave	left	left
become	became	become	lend	lent	lent
begin	began	begun	let	let	let
bend	bent	bent	lie	lay	lain
bite	bit	bitten	light	lit	lit
bleed	bled	bled	lose	lost	lost
blow	blew	blown	make	made	made
break	broke	broken	mean	meant	meant
bring	brought	brought	meet	met	met
build	built	built	pay	paid	paid
burn	burnt	burnt	put	put	put
buy	bought	bought	read	read	read
catch	caught	caught	ride	rode	ridden
choose	chose	chosen	ring	rang	rung
come	came	come	rise	rose	risen
cost	cost	cost	run	ran	run
cut	cut	cut	say	said	said
dig	dug	dug	see	saw	seen
do	did	done	sell	sold	sold
draw	drew	drawn	send	sent	sent
dream	dreamt	dreamt	set	set	set
drink	drank	drunk	shake	shook	shaken
drive	drove	driven	shine	shone	shone
eat	ate	eaten	shoot	shot	shot
fall	fell	fallen	show	showed	shown
feed	fed	fed	shut	shut	shut
feel	felt	felt	sing	sang	sung
fight	fought	fought	sit	sat	sat
find	found	found	sleep	slept	slept
fly	flew	flown	smell	smelt	smelt
forget	forgot	forgotten	speak	spoke	spoken
forgive	forgave	forgiven	spell	spelt	spelt
freeze	froze	frozen	spend	spent	spent
get	got	got	spread	spread	spread
give	gave	given	stand	stood	stood
go	went	gone	steal	stole	stolen
grow	grew	grown	sweep	swept	swept
have	had	had	swim	swam	swum
hear	heard	heard	take	took	taken
hide	hid	hidden	teach	taught	taught
hit	hit	hit	tear	tore	torn
hold	held	held	tell	told	told
hurt	hurt	hurt	think	thought	thought
keep	kept	kept	throw	threw	thrown
know	knew	known	wake	woke	woken
lay	laid	laid	wear	wore	worn
lead	led	led	win	won	won
			write	wrote	written

Keys to Units 1–10

1 1 Personal information

2 Listening (page 6)

1

A
Name: John
Surname: Rose
Address: 24 Walton Road, London
Sex: Male
Age: 16
Occupation: Schoolboy
Interests: Football, tennis, volleyball, listening to music, watching television

B
Name: Amanda
Surname: Wilson
Address: 45 Knight Street, York
Sex: Female
Age: 17
Occupation: Shop assistant
Interests: Horse riding, hill walking, getting out of the city

3 Speaking (page 7)

3

1 Yolanda Brown
2 Yusuf Amiri
3 Angela Beaufort
4 Paolo Mitchell
5 Irina Gallagher

4 Writing (page 7)

1 good football
2 interested in
3 old are
4 do you
5 you spell

6 Listening (page 8)

1 **1** C **2** E **3** F **4** B **5** G

2 A/D

7 Reading (page 8)

1 **1** B **2** C

1 2 A regular thing

1 Vocabulary (page 9)

1

attend: class, meeting
boil: water
brush: hair, pet, shoes, teeth
clean: desk, furniture, shoes, teeth
comb: hair
dial: number
dust: desk, furniture
feed: pet
iron: shirt
miss: bus, class, meeting
tidy: desk, dishes, hair
tie: hair, shoelaces
wash: dishes, hair, pet, shirt

2

hand in: books, homework
join in: game
plug in: light, radio
put away: books, game, homework, make-up, socks, umbrella
put on: light, make-up, music, radio, socks
put up: umbrella
take off: make-up, socks
turn on: light, music, radio
turn up: light, music, radio

2 Reading (page 9)

1 A, B **2** C **3** A **4** C **5** A **6** B, C
7 B **8** A

4 Writing (page 11)

1 as tidy as
2 faster than
3 more comfortable than
4 less homework than
5 worse than

5 Reading (page 11)

2
1 A **2** B **3** D **4** A **5** C **6** C **7** B
8 D **9** A **10** B

2 1 You live and learn

2 Speaking (page 12)

2

Her favourite way of studying Spanish is alone with a text book.

B is the correct picture.

She likes studying in this way because she's good at grammar, and the book has got lots of practice exercises.

3 Speaking (page 14)

2 **1** F **2** E **3** G **4** C **5** A

3 B D

4 Listening (page 14)

1 B **2** B **3** A **4** B **5** A

5 Writing (page 14)

1 is two hours
2 much does
3 in my
4 with
5 about talking

2 2 All the best books

1 Reading (page 15)

a) 2 **b)** 1
a) 1 **b)** 2
1 C **2** B

2 Vocabulary (page 15)

A travel **B** romance **C** humour **D** mystery
E biography **F** thriller **G** horror
H science fiction

3 Reading (page 16)

1 C **2** E **3** B **4** A **5** G

Get ready box (page 17)

2 C and F
   No. A is a novel for teenagers and adults; B is an autobiography for adults; E is a science fiction story for teenagers.
   C or F may be suitable. C is for very young children and F is for children between five and ten years old.
3 C is about animals. F is about space travel.
4 F is unsuitable because it is factual and not a story that Laura can read to her grandson many times. The most suitable book is C, because it is for young children and it's about animals.

4 Vocabulary (page 17)

1–5 Answers will vary.

5 Writing (page 17)

This is the story with the sentences in the correct order.

The Strange Visitor
One day when Jenny arrived home, she saw someone standing at her front door, hidden underneath a large, old-fashioned coat and hat. She didn't know why, but she felt that this person was very old, wise and kind. Although the person didn't speak, Jenny could hear some words in her head. 'This is only my first visit, and when we meet again I will show you my home on a distant planet. To prepare for that day, you must study hard and learn all you can.' Jenny cried out in surprise and the strange visitor disappeared. She knew what she had to do. She went inside, took out her homework and studied all evening.

3 1 Holiday adventures

1 Reading (page 18)

a) 2   **b)** 3   **c)** 1
1 C   **2** B   **3** A

2 Speaking (page 18)

1
1   a girl
2   in her bedroom
3   packing a suitcase
4   a plastic suitcase, clothes, a quilt
5   excited about her holiday; and nervous, because she doesn't know what will happen.

2
Example:
This picture shows a young woman in her bedroom. She's packing some things in a plastic suitcase, which is on her bed. There are some clothes already in the suitcase and some more on the bed. The bed has a pink-and-white quilt and a pillow on it. I think the young woman is going abroad on holiday so she probably feels excited, but perhaps she also feels nervous because she doesn't know what's going to happen.

Extra details may also be given.
Example:
The young woman has long dark hair and she's wearing jeans and a green T-shirt. The bedroom is quite small and doesn't have much furniture apart from the bed. I think the windows are in the ceiling. There may be a cupboard in the room but I can't quite see.

3 Reading (page 19)

2
1 Incorrect   **2** Correct   **3** Correct   **4** Incorrect
5 Incorrect   **6** Correct   **7** Incorrect   **8** Correct
9 Correct   **10** Incorrect

Get ready box (page 20)

2
Sentence 4: The Safari Team
Sentence 6: Good Food
Sentence 9: Quality Camping Equipment
3
Sentence 1: *Every seat is a window seat…*
Sentence 3: *All safari team leaders… have worked for at least a year…*
Sentence 8: *All water carried on the truck is safe… never runs out*
4
No   Yes

4 Writing (page 20)

1   you have learnt
2   soon as
3   we have/we've
4   was on holiday
5   before you book

5 Vocabulary (page 20)

Transport: car, plane, coach, train
Accommodation: hotel, guest house, tent
Scenery: beach, countryside
Activities: swimming, taking photos, sunbathing, picnics
Things to pack: sunglasses, suntan lotion, guidebook
Souvenirs: postcards, shells, handicrafts

3 2 Just the job

1 Reading (page 21)

1 C   **2** A

2 Vocabulary (page 21)

1

Profession	Subject studied
architect	architecture
doctor	medicine
lawyer	law
artist	art
cook	cookery/cooking
engineer	engineering
tourist guide	tourism
hairdresser	hairdressing
journalist	journalism
businesswoman	business
actor	acting
chemist	chemistry
biologist	biology
physicist	physics
musician	music

2

Verb	Noun
apply	application
organize	organization
qualify	qualification
decide	decision
operate	operation
employ	employment
advertise	advertisement
govern	government
manage	management
retire	retirement
insure	insurance
succeed	success

3 Listening (page 22)

1

Speaker 1: uniform, car, city centre, controlling traffic.
Speaker 2: jeans, computer, advertising agency, drawing.
Speaker 3: white coat, microscope, zoo, testing.
Speaker 4: suit, phone, bank, helping customers.
1 C   **2** A   **3** D   **4** B
2
1 C   **2** B   **3** C   **4** B   **5** A   **6** A

4 1 House and home

1 Vocabulary (page 24)
2

Living room: coffee table, armchair, television, lamp, sofa
Kitchen: dishwasher, sink, fridge, cooker
Bathroom: washbasin, shower, towel rail, mirror
Bedroom: wardrobe, chest of drawers, dressing table, television, lamp, mirror

3 Listening (page 25)

1   C

5 Listening (page 26)

1   C
2   B
3   C
4   C

4 2 Interesting people

1 Vocabulary (page 27)

3
attractive/ugly   careful/careless
cheerful/miserable   confident/shy
foolish/wise   hard-working/lazy
strong/weak
4
amusing/funny   anxious/worried
blond/fair   boring/dull
understanding/patient   honest/truthful
slim/thin
5
Answers will depend on the students.

3 Reading (page 28)

1
1 D   **2** C   **3** A   **4** B   **5** C
2
1 C   **2** E   **3** B   **4** D   **5** A

4 Writing (page 29)

1   who is
2   strong enough
3   many students have
4   more than/better than
5   (the) best/(the) most

5 1 Places of interest

1 Reading (page 30)

1
1   post office
2   sports centre
3   hotel
4   giftshop
5   post office
6   museum
7   sports centre
8   giftshop
9   hotel
10   museum
2
1 c)   **2** c)   **3** b)   **4** a)   **5** b)
6 b)   **7** a)   **8** b)   **9** a)   **10** a)
3
Example answers:
School:
a) Packed lunches are now available from the canteen.
b) Shoes must not be worn in the hall.
c) The school bus leaves from the main entrance.
Department store:
a) The coffee shop is open on the fifth floor.
b) This lift holds up to five people.
c) Sale begins Friday January 4th.
Bank:
a) New Savings Account 5% per annum.
b) Please wait here until a cashier is free.
c) This branch is open on Saturdays 10.00–13.00.
Airport:
a) Zone A: Check-in for domestic flights
b) Please keep your baggage with you at all times.
c) BA 244 London: Please go to gate 16.

2 Listening (page 31)

1
1 10.00 am
2 £1.20
3 450472
2
1 November
2 6.00 pm
3 old walls
4 museum
3
1 Wednesday
2 leaflet
3 poster

3 Reading (page 32)

1 Incorrect   **2** Incorrect   **3** Correct   **4** Incorrect
5 Correct   **6** Incorrect   **7** Correct   **8** Incorrect
9 Correct   **10** Correct

5 2 Getting there

1 Vocabulary (page 33)

1
Taxi: driver, catch, fare, take, meter
Train: driver, catch, miss, get on, ticket, fare,
station, take, platform, timetable
Bus/coach: driver, catch, miss, get on, ticket, fare,
station, take, timetable
Plane: pilot, attendant, land, catch, miss, get on,
take off, check in, ticket, fare, gate, take, boarding
pass, timetable
2
1 miss, station
2 catch/take, fare, tickets
3 check in, boarding pass, gate, get on
4 platform, ticket, get on
5 timetable, catch

3 Reading (page 34)

1
A taxi   **B** train   **C** plane
D bus/coach   **E** bus/coach
2 C
3
1 C   **2** C   **3** C   **4** A   **5** C

6 1 What a bargain!

2 Reading (page 36)

1 D
2 A
3 C

3 Vocabulary (page 36)

1 earn, save   **2** cheque, credit   **3** note, coin
4 receipt, owe   **5** lend   **6** shop   **7** charge
8 tip

4 Writing (page 37)

2
1 for
2 with
3 it/that
4 is
5 and/or
6 for
7 have
8 go
9 on
10 we
11 going
12 spend
13 the
14 a
15 me

Topic: shopping, in both letters
Different kinds of shopping: food, clothes, CDs
Angela's reasons for disliking food shopping are
   'The supermarket is always crowded' and *'it's
   boring'.*
Angela's examples of things she does when
   shopping are trying on clothes and not buying
   anything, and spending hours listening to the
   latest CDs.
Angela's 'hello' sentence: *'Thank you for your
   letter.'*
Angela's 'goodbye' sentence: *'Please write to me
   again soon.'*
Other 'hello' sentences: *'I'm sorry I haven't written
   for a long time.' 'I was really pleased to hear your
   news.' 'It was great to hear from you again.'* The
   rest are 'goodbye' sentences.

5 Listening (page 38)

1 flowers   **2** leather jackets
3 Sunday   **4** a hospital

6 2 City life

2 Speaking (page 39)

2

Answers will vary; some words can be used more than once.

a) the city: crowded, noisy, dirty, stressful, convenient, expensive, exciting, lonely, interesting, fun, dangerous, polluted.

b) the country: calm, peaceful, clean, boring, relaxing, safe, lonely, interesting, fun, inconvenient.

3

Some words can be used more than once.

a) the city: shopping, night-life, way of life, education, employment, transport, entertainment.

b) the country: fresh air, way of life, education, health.

7 1 Food and drink

1 Vocabulary (page 42)

1

Meat and fish: lamb, sausages, duck, beef, chicken, tuna, steak, burgers

Vegetables: carrots, beans, peas, onions, garlic, mushrooms, tomatoes, leeks, olives, spinach

Fruit: bananas, grapes, oranges, plums

Other: pasta, rice, mayonnaise, butter, cheese, pepper, salt, pizza

2 Speaking (page 42)

3

The topic of the conversation is food that you eat when you go out and when you stay at home.

3 Vocabulary (page 44)

1

some different-sized tomatoes
a small tin of tuna fish
two spoonfuls of mayonnaise
a hard-boiled egg
some black olives
two spoonfuls of tomato sauce
You need: a mixing bowl, a fork and spoon, and a fairly sharp knife.

2

	Equipment	Verb	Ingredients
1	knife	cut	tomatoes
2	spoon	take out	seeds
3	mixing bowl	put in	tuna and egg
4	fork	mix	tuna and egg
5	spoon	stir in	mayonnaise and tomato sauce
6	spoon	put	mixture into tomatoes
7	knife	cut up	tomatoes and olives

4 Writing (page 44)

1 usually prepares
2 finished all the
3 me not to
4 I have
5 order

7 2 Your own space

2 Reading (page 45)

1

1 B	2 C	3 B	4 C	5 B
6 D	7 A	8 D	9 B	10 C

2

1 C	2 B	3 B

3 Listening (page 46)

2

1 A	2 B	3 B	4 A	5 A	6 B

5 Listening (page 47)

1 A	2 B	3 A	4 A	5 B	6 B

8 1 Close to nature

1 Vocabulary (page 48)

1 destroying	2 breathe	3 dusty
4 spoil	5 rubbish	6 minerals
7 fuels	8 poverty	9 prevent
10 rescue	11 urgent	12 inhabitants

2 Listening (page 48)

1

Speaker 1 B   **Speaker 2** C   **Speaker 3** A

2

Good weather: fine, clear, warm, sunshine, hot, sunny, dry up

Bad weather: storms, thunder, lightning, snow, frost, mist, clouds, wind, rain, snow-covered, freezing, foggy, dull, damp, changeable, shower, pouring, cooler, gales
Other weather words: forecast, slipping

4 Reading (page 49)

1 A **2** C **3** D **4** B **5** D
6 A **7** B **8** C **9** B **10** A

5 Listening (page 50)

1 C **2** A **3** C **4** B **5** B **6** A

8 2 The wide world

1 Reading (page 51)

2
1 Incorrect **2** Correct **3** Incorrect
4 Correct **5** Correct

2 Vocabulary (page 52)

1

1 *desert* because it's not a word for a high place
2 *waterfall* because it's not an area of land
3 *island* because it doesn't mean a place with a lot of trees
4 *cave* because it's not water
5 *bay* because it's not a kind of earth
6 *wave* because you can't walk down it
7 *valley* because it's not part of the coastline
8 *flood* because it doesn't describe the limit of something

4 Writing (page 53)

1
1 far from
2 (ever) going for
3 you look at
4 have been
5 you like to

2
1 took
2 as/so heavy as
3 difficult for
4 find/have found
5 so has

5 Reading (page 53)

1 A **2** C

9 1 Free time

1 Vocabulary (page 54)

1
1 windsurfing
2 table-tennis
3 golf
4 gymnastics
5 judo
6 hockey
7 baseball

2 Reading (page 54)

1 F **2** A **3** D **4** G **5** C

3 Vocabulary (page 56)

1

1 material, needle, scissors, pins, refreshing drink
2 brush, hammer, nails, paint, refreshing drink
3 dictionary, envelope, notepaper, stamp, refreshing drink
4 flower pot, watering can, seeds, spade, refreshing drink
5 balls, net, racket, sports bag, refreshing drink

9 2 Get well soon!

2 Vocabulary (page 57)

1 emergency, accident, ambulance
2 earache, clinic, pill, pain
3 deaf
4 nurse, patient
5 drug, fit
6 ill, sore, cough, flu
7 wound, pale, dizzy, faint

3 Reading (page 58)

1 D **2** A **3** D **4** B **5** C

4 Writing (page 59)

1 my head was
2 keep fit
3 you give up
4 have (got)
5 can't/shouldn't/may not/mustn't smoke

10 1 Entertainment

1 Speaking (page 60)

2

curtain: theatre, concert
interval: concert, theatre, cinema
ticket: cinema, concert, theatre, clubbing
encore: concert, theatre
soap opera: television
channel: television
website: the Internet
programme: television, concert, theatre
soloist: concert
commercial: television, cinema
backing group: concert
chat room: the Internet

2 Vocabulary (page 60)

1

1 series   **2** part   **3** lines   **4** rehearsal
5 stage   **6** clap   **7** reviews   **8** studio
9 camera   **10** director   **11** performance
12 screen

2
1 C   **2** A
3
1 journalist   **2** plays

3 Listening (page 61)

1 B

2 C

3 A

5 Listening (page 62)

1 8.15/eight fifteen
2 drummer
3 weather forecast
4 wild flowers
5 *The Cookery Programme*
6 *Happy Times*

10 2 The age of communication

2 Reading (page 65)

1 B   **2** C   **3** A   **4** D   **5** B
6 B   **7** A   **8** B   **9** D   **10** C

3 Writing (page 65)

1   than (using)
2   confuses/is confusing for
3   belong
4   tired
5   I would/I'd

Key to Practice Test 1

Paper 1 Reading and Writing

Page 66 Reading PART 1
1 B   2 A   3 B   4 C   5 C

Page 67 Reading PART 2
6 C   7 A   8 E   9 G   10 H

Page 68 Reading PART 3
11 A   12 B   13 A   14 A   15 B   16 B
17 A   18 B   19 B   20 B

Page 69 Reading PART 4
21 C   22 D   23 A   24 B   25 C

Page 70 Reading PART 5
26 B   27 C   28 A   29 D   30 D
31 A   32 C   33 B   34 B   35 C

Page 71 Writing PART 1
1   found
2   well
3   as patient as
4   until/till
5   let me borrow/lend me

Page 71 Writing PART 2
There are 5 marks for this part. To get 5 marks, the answer should include these points:

- thanks for the evening at Chris' house
- mention of something particularly enjoyable about the evening
- an invitation to Chris

More information about how this part is assessed is given on pages 121–124.

Page 72 Writing PART 3
There are 15 marks for this part.
Information about how this part is assessed is given on pages 121–124.

Paper 2 Listening

Page 73 Listening PART 1
1 B   2 B   3 A   4 C   5 C   6 B   7 B

Page 74 Listening PART 2
8 A   9 C   10 B   11 C   12 A   13 C

Page 74 Listening PART 3
14   (some) videos
15   watersports
16   £850
17   May
18   (the) US dollar(s)
19   tourist card

Page 75 Listening PART 4
20 A   21 B   22 A   23 B   24 A   25 B

> **Note:** the Practice Tests are sample tests only, and are not actual UCLES past papers.

Key to Practice Test 2

Paper 1 Reading and Writing

Page 79 Reading PART 1
1 B　2 A　3 C　4 C　5 B

Page 80 Reading PART 2
6 G　7 A　8 F　9 C　10 H

Page 81 Reading PART 3
11 B　12 B　13 A　14 B　15 A
16 B　17 B　18 A　19 A　20 A

Page 82 Reading PART 4
21 B　22 D　23 D　24 A　25 C

Page 83 Reading PART 5
26 B　27 C　28 A　29 D　30 D
31 C　32 A　33 B　34 C　35 B

Page 84 Writing PART 1
1　had
2　have collected/have been collecting
3　an expensive
4　learn/know/find out
5　most valuable

Page 84 Writing PART 2
There are 5 marks for this part. To get 5 marks, the answer should include these points:

• the name of the subject being studied
• some information about the teacher
• an expression of feeling about the subject

More information about how this part is assessed is given on pages 121–124.

Page 85 Writing PART 3
There are 15 marks for this part.
Information about how this part is assessed is given on pages 121–124.

Paper 2 Listening

Page 86 Listening PART 1
1 C　2 B　3 A　4 C　5 A　6 A　7 C

Page 87 Listening PART 2
8 A　9 B　10 B　11 A　12 C　13 C

Page 87 Listening PART 3
14　£47.50
15　action (films/movies)
16　(first week of) June
17　wildlife
18　horror (films/movies)
19　cartoons

Page 88 Listening PART 4
20 A　21 B　22 B　23 A　24 A　25 B

Note: the Practice Tests are sample tests only, and are not actual UCLES past papers.

Tapescripts for Units 1–10

1 1 Personal information

2 Listening (page 6)

1

A Hello. My name is John, that's J O H N. And my surname is Rose, that's R O S E. I would like to give you some information about myself. First of all, I live in London and my address is 24, Walton Road. That's Walton W A L T O N, Walton Road in London. So, what else can I tell you? I'm a 16-year-old boy and so I'm still at school and I'm *very* interested in sport. I'm quite good at football and I also enjoy playing tennis and volleyball. When I'm not playing sport, I like listening to music and watching television.

B Hello. My name's Amanda Wilson and you spell my first name A M A N D A, Amanda and my surname is Wilson, which is spelt W I L S O N. My name's not really difficult to spell, but people always make mistakes in my address. I live in York, that's Y O R K, at 45 Knight Street which is spelt K N I G H T Street. I'm a 17-year-old English girl and I work as a shop assistant in a large shop in my home city. In my free time, I like to get out of the city, however, and I'm very interested in horse riding and hill walking. I'm not very good at horse riding yet because I only started last year, but I've been hill walking since I was 12 years old. I love it.

3 Speaking (page 7)

3

1 My name is Yolanda Brown. That's YOLANDA BROWN.
2 My name is Yusuf Amiri. That's YUSUF AMIRI.
3 My name is Angela Beaufort. That's ANGELA BEAUFORT.
4 My name is Paolo Mitchell. That's PAOLO MITCHELL.
5 My name is Irina Gallagher. That's IRINA GALLAGHER.

6 Listening (page 8)

2

David: Hello. I'm David.
Victoria: Hi. I'm Victoria. I'm a friend of Tom's from college.
David: Yes, I'm one of his friends too, and we play football together. What do you study?
Victoria: I'm doing languages. What about you?
David: I've finished college, actually, and I'm working as a windsurfing instructor.
Victoria: Oh, I'm really interested in watersports, but I'm not very good at windsurfing.
David: That doesn't matter. You could learn.
Victoria: Yes, I suppose so. But what I'm really interested in is sailing.
David: So am I. I'm running a course which starts next week. Would you be interested in joining?
Victoria: Oh... I might be... it depends.

2 1 You live and learn

2 Speaking (page 12)

2

Boy: Hello, Polly. How are your Spanish classes going?

Polly: Oh, OK. The teacher's very nice, but the classes are a bit boring. I really like studying on my own, you know. My dad bought me a Spanish CD for my computer, but actually I prefer the textbook because I'm good at grammar, and the book has got lots of practice exercises. One day, I'd like to be able to listen and understand the words to Spanish pop music, but I'm not good enough for that yet!

3 Speaking (page 14)

3

Valerie: So, our friend wants to learn a new language?

Pietro: That's right, and he's only got £20 to spend, so he can't buy all these things, can he?

Valerie: No, he can't. Let's start by talking about which of them will be useful for him.

Pietro: OK, then afterwards we can decide which one he should buy.

Valerie: OK. Shall we start with this one, the dictionary?

Pietro: Yes, I think he should buy one of those, because it's very useful if you don't know what words mean.

Valerie: Yes, I agree, and it's also good for checking spelling. But what about a textbook? They're useful too.

Pietro: Yes they are, but maybe he won't need one because he'll have a teacher.

Valerie: Possibly. Or he may get one free when he pays for the course.

Pietro: Oh yes, that's a good point.

4 Listening (page 14)

Tim: Hi Janet. How's your computer course going?

Janet: Oh, I've just had my class, actually. We have them twice a week and each one lasts two hours.

Tim: Gosh. That's long. Doesn't it get boring?

Janet: Well, you need that long to actually do a whole document. It's really good because I can do all sorts of things on my computer that I never even knew existed before.

Tim: I can't say the same for my cookery course.

Janet: Oh, Tim, why not? I thought you were enjoying it.

Tim: Oh it's enjoyable enough, but we just don't seem to make much progress. We spent the whole of last week's lesson learning how to fry an egg.

Janet: Well, it's not an easy thing to do properly, you know.

Tim: Oh I know, but I don't even like eggs.

Janet: Oh poor Tim! So ... how often is it?

Tim: Just once a week, for an hour and a half.

Janet: And do you get to eat all the things you make?

Tim: Well, you're not meant to eat them there, but you can take them home because you have to buy all the stuff in the first place. It's cakes next week.

Janet: Oh, that sounds fun!

Tim: Oh yes. I'm looking forward to it. But Janet, I wanted to ask you something, actually. Have you learnt how to send e-mails on your course yet?

Janet: Oh yes, we did that in the first week.

Tim: Because I can't get my computer to send them properly, and I was wondering if you'd show me how it's done?

Janet: Well, if you bring me one of your cakes, I suppose I could try.

Tim: Great, well, when I've made them...

3 2 Just the job

3 Listening (page 22)

1

1

I love what I do and I'm very proud of the uniform I wear. I drive around for most of the day but I'm always somewhere in the city centre. My job is controlling the traffic. When I hear there's a traffic problem I go and see what I can do about it. I just use my hands and my voice – no equipment's necessary – except for my car, of course. I couldn't work without that!

2

I never did well at school. I was only interested in drawing – I was quite good at that. And that's what I do now – drawing. I work in an advertising agency and I do the artwork for advertisements. But I don't use a pencil or paint – it's all done on a computer – that's the only piece of equipment I need. I like being comfortable when I work, so I wear jeans. I don't even own a suit.

3

This is my first job and I've only been here for a year. My microscope is my most important piece of equipment. I couldn't do my work here in the zoo without it. I love animals but I don't often get to see the ones here! My job is testing. I test all kinds of things – the animals' food, the water they drink, and if they get ill, I test their blood. It's very important that everything here is clean, so I have to wear a white coat over my clothes, and I'm always washing my hands!

4

Actually, I want to change what I do. I work in a bank, and it's a good job, but I'd like to do something more exciting. Here it's the same thing every day. My job is helping customers. I help customers when they come into the bank and I help them when they phone up. I don't really have any equipment apart from the phone. I spend a lot of time on the phone. I have to wear a suit at work, which I hate – I'd much prefer to wear jeans!

2

Presenter: ...and today in our series about people who work for themselves, we have Amanda Turner. Good morning, Amanda. Tell us what you do.

Amanda: Well, basically I'm a cook. Unlike most cooks, who work at home or in a restaurant, I'm employed by various recording studios. When musicians are making an album, they have to stay in the studio all day, so I go there and prepare meals for them.

Presenter: Are musicians hard to please?

Amanda: Fortunately, they seem to be satisfied with what I do. When they're recording, they want something tasty but quite simple. They don't want to eat a lot, or be given unfamiliar dishes. The food has to be good for them because they're always worried about getting ill, or putting on weight.

Presenter: Would you call it a stressful job?

Amanda: It isn't usually. I only get worried when they forget to tell me how many people will want to eat, or when they tell me to expect five for a meal and then fifteen hungry people arrive! Often I don't have a proper kitchen to work in, and sometimes the meal is ready long before the musicians have finished playing. But I don't mind that.

Presenter: You're happy in your work, then?

Amanda: Oh, yes. I know I'm lucky to do what I enjoy, and to get paid well for it. And I meet all sorts of interesting people! Think of your favourite boy band, and I've probably cooked them a meal! But I work with all kinds of musicians, pop and classical, famous and unknown, young and old. I'm happiest when I'm cooking for the young ones. They always *really* enjoy my food and say nice things about it.

Presenter: So how long is a typical day?

Amanda: *Very* long! I walk round the market early in the morning, buying vegetables and fresh meat and fish. I have to be at the studios by noon. I don't drive, and anyway it's always difficult to park, so they send a car to pick me up. Going on the bus with all my bags of shopping would be terrible! After cooking, serving and clearing up, I never get home before nine in the evening. My daughter prepares a snack for us while I tell her about the day's music. I also do a cookery page for a monthly magazine, so before I go to bed, I do some work on that. I always sleep really well!

Presenter: It sounds like a busy life! Thanks for talking to us, Amanda.

4 1 House and home

3 Listening (page 25)

1

In my room, there's not much furniture. I've got a bed, of course, but I don't have a wardrobe because I keep all my clothes in a chest of drawers. My parents don't like me putting posters on the wall, and for a long time I didn't have any, but I've recently been allowed to put up one or two. My parents bought me a desk to do my homework on, but I don't use it much. I like my room. It's nice.

5 Listening (page 26)

1

Boy:	Mum, I can't find my calculator.
Mum:	Isn't it on your bedside table?
Boy:	I've looked there and in the chest of drawers, but it's not there.
Mum:	I saw a lot of things pushed under the bed when I was cleaning yesterday. It's probably there. If not, have you looked in the wardrobe?
Boy:	Oh, it's OK. I've found it on the floor like you said. But I don't understand how it got there!

2

Man:	Excuse me, I've just missed the 3.35 bus. Can you tell me what time the next one leaves?
Woman:	Certainly sir. There's a bus to London at 3.45 and one to Manchester at 4.35.
Man:	Oh. I wanted the London bus, actually. I didn't think it would be so soon.
Woman:	Yes, there's one at 3.45 and then another at 4.45. But there wasn't one at 3.35, that one was going to Edinburgh, so you haven't missed it really.

3

Waiter:	Would you like to order, madam? Today's soup is tomato, or we have some cheese and tomato pizza. The other pizzas are all finished, I'm afraid.
Woman:	Oh, that's a shame. I want more than a sandwich, but I didn't want to eat too much. Umm... OK then, I'll have chicken and chips, please.
Waiter:	I'm sorry, the chicken's finished, but we could do you a burger?
Woman:	Oh, really? In that case I'd rather have a sandwich, just plain cheese, please.

4

Woman:	Hello, I've come to cut Susie's hair for her.
Man:	Oh yes, come in. She's expecting you.
Woman:	I wasn't sure what to bring. I've brought some special shampoo she might like to try, it's very good, and I've got scissors and a comb. But if she wants her hair washed, I might need to borrow something to dry it with, because I'm thinking of blow-drying it.
Man:	Oh... I'm afraid we haven't got a hairdryer, but I can give you a towel if you want.

5 1 Places of interest

2 Listening (page 31)

1

Hello. This is the Orford Castle Information Line. Orford Castle is an 800-year-old building which is located near the sea at Orford in the east of England. The castle opens every day at 10.00 am, and stays open until four o'clock in the afternoon. It takes about one hour to look around the castle and you can climb a spiral staircase to the top of the tower, which is 30 metres high. From there, you can see for miles. Admission prices are as follows: adults £2.30 and children £1.20. Children receive a free Activity Sheet and can find out more about the castle in the interactive CD ROM unit. A full-colour souvenir guide is also available. For more information about Orford Castle, phone 01394 450472 during office hours. Thank you for calling the Orford Castle Information Line.

2

Hello and welcome to the Framlingham Castle Information Line. Framlingham Castle is open between the months of April and November. The castle dates back to the 12th century and from the outside looks much as it did 800 years ago. The castle opens at 10.00 am and closes at 6.00 pm. Once inside the castle, most people walk around the old walls, from where you get a wonderful view of the surrounding countryside, but there are also a number of other things to see and do. There is also a museum to visit, where you can get lots of information about the castle's history, and a fully interactive audio tour is available for adults and children alike. Admission costs £2.95 for adults and £1.50 for children. Thank you for calling the Framlingham Castle Information line.

3

Hello and welcome to the Castle Rising Information Line. Castle Rising is open to the public from Wednesday to Sunday each week at this time of year, opening at 10.00 am and closing at 3.30 in the afternoon. Admission costs £2.30 for adults and £1.70 for children. When you enter the castle, you will be given a free leaflet giving you information about its history, and explaining what you can see as you walk round. It takes about an hour to visit the castle, but if the weather's nice, you can bring a picnic to eat in the park and stay as long as you like. There is a small giftshop at the castle where you can buy a souvenir poster to remind you of your visit. We look forward to seeing you at Castle Rising. Thank you for calling.

6 1 What a bargain!

5 Listening (page 38)

This is Radio London Fun calling all tourists in London! Did you know that East London has some of the most interesting street markets in Europe?

First up, there's Columbia Road market. You can buy flowers here at any one of 50 stalls. And whatever flowers you choose, they won't cost you much!

Next, there's Brick Lane market. Not everything here is new, but there's something for everybody. And if you're looking for a really good souvenir of London, then check out this market's speciality, leather jackets. You'll have to try one on!

Then, there's Petticoat Lane Market, the oldest and most famous of all London's markets. Buy anything here, from fashionable clothes to toys for the children. Come any morning from Monday to Friday, or on Sunday, when the market is at its biggest and most crowded.

Finally, there's Whitechapel market. It's easy to get to because it's right by the underground station, and just across the road from a hospital. This is the place to buy exotic vegetables and spices from Asia.

So, get down to East London now and be part of the fun!

7 1 Food and drink

2 Speaking (page 43)

3

Examiner: Your photographs showed people eating a meal. Now I'd like you to talk together about the type of food you eat when you go out and when you stay at home.

4

Examiner: Your photographs showed people eating a meal. Now I'd like you to talk together about the type of food you eat when you go out and when you stay at home.

Girl: So, Tom, do you often eat out?

Tom: Sometimes... sometimes I go out for a meal with my family, and sometimes I go with my friends. What about you?

Girl: Yes, me too. What type of restaurant does your family go to?

Tom: Different types, but usually traditional ones. They like to have steak and chips and things like that, but I prefer Italian food...

Girl: Really! So do I. It's much more interesting than English food, isn't it?

Tom: Yes, I agree with you about that, and another thing is that it isn't very expensive.

Girl: That's right. When I go out with my friends, I always go to either an Italian or a Chinese restaurant.

Tom: Yes, me too... and also Thai... have you tried Thai food?

Girl: No, what's it like?

Tom: Well, it's similar to Chinese, but it has different tastes and unusual vegetables.

Girl: Oh, that sounds good!

Tom: Yes, you should try it.

3 Vocabulary (page 44)

1

I'm going to tell you how to make tomato owls. First of all, you need some different-sized tomatoes, some big ones and some smaller ones, and a small tin of tuna fish. As well as these two main ingredients, you also need two spoonfuls of mayonnaise, a hard-boiled egg, and some black olives. To give colour, you will also need two spoonfuls of tomato sauce.

You don't have to cook the owls, but to make them you do need some basic equipment. Firstly, you need a mixing bowl to make the mixture in. To make the mixture you need a fork and a spoon, and to cut up the tomatoes and olives you need a fairly sharp knife.

2

So, now I'm going to tell you how to make the tomato owls. Firstly, take the knife and cut the tomatoes in half. Then take the spoon and use it to take the seeds out of the middle of the tomatoes, so that there's a hole for the mixture to go in. Then put the tuna and the hard-boiled egg into the mixing bowl. Then, using a fork, mix them together. When you have a good mixture, stir in the mayonnaise and the tomato sauce, using a spoon. Now take some of the mixture on the spoon and put it into the bottom half of each tomato. Cut the remaining tomato pieces into triangles to make the owl's mouth and ears, and cut up an olive to make its eyes.

7 2 Your own space

3 Listening (page 46)

2

Bob: Hello, Mary, how are you?

Mary: Oh, hello Bob. Not too bad. We're having one or two problems with our son Matthew.

Bob: Really? What sort of problems?

Mary: Well, he wants to have his own bedroom, but we haven't got the space and he doesn't seem to understand.

Bob: Oh, so he shares with his brother, does he?

Mary: Yes, but there's not a great age difference, just one year, so you'd think they'd be able to get on together, wouldn't you?

Bob: I remember I used to hate sharing a bedroom with my older brother. We used to argue all the time. Mostly about privacy, as I remember.

Mary: Privacy? You mean you wanted more time to be alone?

Bob: It wasn't that. It was more that I wanted to have my own space. You know, we had one wardrobe, one chest of drawers. I didn't even have one drawer that was all mine, and so my elder brother used to just take all my things if he fancied them.

Mary: Oh, I see. I wonder if that's Matthew's problem? Because he wanted his own computer, but there's not room for two in the one small bedroom, so we said no, they'd have to share.

Bob: So who gets to use it all the time?

Mary: I don't know, but they always seem to be fighting about something, and of course Matthew doesn't have as much homework as his brother, so maybe he doesn't need it so much.

Bob: Well, they're not only for doing homework on, you know.

Mary: I know that Bob, and they've got their own television in the room, but Matthew doesn't really seem to like television very much. I don't understand him sometimes.

Bob: Well, maybe it's because he doesn't get to watch the programmes he likes.

Mary: Actually, I think he'd rather not have the television in the room. I think I'd better talk to them about these things. Maybe we can arrange things better. Thanks Bob.

Bob: Don't mention it.

5 Listening (page 47)

Alice: Oh, hello Harry, how are you?

Harry: Fine, thanks. But you look a bit miserable. What's the matter?

Alice: I've been arguing with my mum again, I'm afraid. I feel sorry about it afterwards, but she just annoys me *so much*.

Harry: Yeah, I know what you mean. But what have you been arguing about?

Alice: Oh, the usual thing about my bedroom.

Harry: Your bedroom?

Alice: Yeah. She's always telling me to tidy it up, but it's my room, so I don't see why I should have to.

Harry: And is it really untidy, or is it just that she's *really* fussy about things like that?

Alice: Oh, it's untidy all right. I mean, you know, I take my clothes off at night and just leave them where they fall.

Harry: And you expect your mum to tidy up after you?

Alice: No. I do it sooner or later because it's not good for your stuff to be left screwed up in a ball, is it? It's just that she wants it done like *now*, and I'm happy to leave it for a while and do it later, you know, when I feel like it, or when I've got friends coming round.

Harry: And so you argue?

Alice: Yeah. She wants me to put everything back in the wardrobe, but I've got so much stuff that it won't all fit anyway.

Harry: You're lucky. I have to share a wardrobe with my brother. He's always wearing my things without asking me.

Alice: But don't you each have your own bedroom?

Harry: We do, but his is very small and you can't get a wardrobe in, so he's always coming in and out of my room to get stuff out of it.

Alice: Oh, I wouldn't like that.

Harry: Nor do I. It leads to *lots* of arguments.

8 1 Close to nature

2 Listening (page 48)

1

1

I listened to the weather forecast before we set out and it wasn't encouraging – storms with thunder and lightning and even snow on the hills! Actually, it was a fine, clear day. There was frost on the ground when I woke up and some mist over the fields, but that soon disappeared in the warm sunshine. There were some clouds about, but the wind kept them moving and it didn't rain. All in all, it was a brilliant day!

2

It was lucky we didn't have far to walk on Saturday. I couldn't help slipping on the snow-covered pavements and the air was freezing! But, really, I like that kind of weather best. It kind of makes me feel alive – not like foggy days, or dull, damp ones when I just want to stay indoors, or very hot and sunny ones which send me to sleep! So it was a great day!

3

You know what they say about the weather being changeable? Well, it wasn't like that on Saturday! It was one heavy shower after another – just when we thought it was going to dry up, it started pouring again! Still, it was quite warm, though it got cooler in the evening, so we didn't really mind. I heard later there were gales on the coast, so we escaped them! In spite of the weather, we really enjoyed our day!

5 Listening (page 50)

I've collected several extraordinary animal stories, and I'd like to tell you some of them.

One day, Daisy the cow was peacefully eating grass. Suddenly, a very strong wind blew her up into the air and carried her two kilometres, before landing her safely in a neighbour's field. But that wasn't Daisy's only flight. Five years later, passengers in a bus were amazed to watch as another strong wind lifted Daisy into the air, carried her over their heads, and brought her down on the other side of the road.

You think that's strange? Well, what about Speedy, the cat, and her love of travelling fast? Speedy loves riding on the back of her owner's motorbike and overtaking buses and bicycles. Speedy's owner had to stop her riding on the roof of his car, because it's too dangerous, and he makes her wear a special hard hat for protection when she's on the motorbike.

Another extraordinary cat is Fluffy. Once, when Fluffy was a passenger on a plane, she travelled with the luggage but she escaped from her box. The flight attendants tried to catch her and so did the pilot, but without success. Fluffy travelled backwards and forwards between New York and Los Angeles for 12 days before her owner got her to come out for a nice piece of fish.

Then there's Tom Johnson's pet bird, a pigeon called Pete. Tom drives thousands of kilometres a year, and Pete flies with him. He rides on a stream of air beside the right-hand window of the car, which gives him high speed for little effort, a bit like surfing on a wave. Tom gets anxious that other cars might hit Pete when they pass him, but, apart from that, they both enjoy the long journeys.

Now let me tell you about Rambo, the gorilla. Rambo lives in a zoo and one day a little boy somehow fell into the gorillas' cage. He was hurt and couldn't get up. Rambo made noises to stop the other gorillas coming near the boy, and when he cried, he gently dried the boy's tears with his hand. The way he kept the boy safe has made Rambo famous.

And, finally, let me tell you about another animal that rescued a child. Prince, the dog, lived in a forest on a mountain. One day, he found a little boy half-frozen under a deep pile of snow. He used the heat from his body and his warm tongue to unfreeze the child, and then he carried him on his back to the nearest house.

Well, you must agree, animals can be just amazing!

10 1 Entertainment

3 Listening (page 61)

1

Man: What do you feel like doing tonight? I'm getting a bit tired of clubbing.

Woman: Yeah, me too. How about going to the open-air concert? The guitarist is meant to be *really* good.

Man: Oh, I heard that all the tickets were sold out weeks ago, but there's a good film on at the ABC. You know, it's the one that won all the Oscars.

Woman: OK, and if we can't get in, there's always the theatre next door. That's never full, so it's a good idea.

2

Woman: It's *great*, this new cinema! *Four* films on at the same time, and they're all good.

Man: Well, I don't know about that. There's a good thriller on in Screen Number One, or I wouldn't mind seeing the science fiction one, that's meant to be really good.

Woman: Well, I'm not keen on seeing either of those. But how about the one about animals, that's much more my sort of thing than the other one... what is it? Some sort of romantic comedy?

Man: That's right. Oh well, I'm quite happy to go along with your choice.

3

Man: So, what did you think of it?

Woman: Well, he's a brilliant director, isn't he? All those lovely scenes in the mountains... the camerawork was *wonderful*.

Man: I thought the actors were good on the whole, although to be honest, I think the storyline, the plot, is *so* strong that you don't worry so much about the characters. I mean, it is a classic action film, isn't it?

Woman: I *absolutely* agree with you. I was on the edge of my seat the whole time! You never knew what was going to happen next. That's what *really* made it for me.

Man: Oh yeah, me too.

5 Listening (page 62)

It's now five to eight and there's just time for one more song before the news, but before I do that, I'd just like to tell you about one or two things coming up later today on your local radio station.

First of all, after the eight o'clock news, at 8.15, we have our *Arts Review* programme. Debbie Clarke will be telling you about what's on in the region in the coming week, including information about theatre, cinema and concerts. Today Debbie will also have a special guest in the studio, Kevin Jones, who is the drummer with the very successful pop band, *Splodge*. Kevin will be talking about what it's like to be the drummer rather than the lead singer in a pop band.

That's followed at 8.45 by the weather forecast. Graham Smith will be here to tell you if it's going to be wet or fine for the rest of the week. Let's hope that Graham has some good news for us. After that, at 8.50, a new series begins. Polly Brown has been out and about in the countryside this week talking to people who are interested in wild flowers. And I must say that some of those people really know a great deal about the subject.

After that, at 9.30, we have *The Cookery Programme*. James Grant will be back with some more delicious recipes, and he'll also be telling us what to look out for when we're buying fresh fruit and vegetables. And finally, at 10.15, we have this morning's radio play. *Happy Times* it's called, and it tells the story of two children's summer holiday by the seaside and something which happened that was to change their lives forever. Sounds good. So, that's it on your favourite station today. Now up to the news here is *Splodge* with their latest single, which is called '*Take me*'.

Tapescript for Practice Test 1

Practice Test 1 - Paper 2 Listening

Page 73   PART 1

RUBRIC = R

R There are seven questions in this part. For each question there are three pictures and a short recording. Choose the correct picture and put a tick in the box below it.

Before we start, here is an example.

R Where did the man leave his sunglasses?

M Oh no! I've lost my sunglasses.

F Well, you had them on in the car. Perhaps you left them inside?

M No, I remember taking them off when we parked outside the restaurant. Perhaps I left them in there, or in that shop we went into, just before we had lunch.

F No, you didn't leave them in the shop, because you put them on the table while we were eating. They must still be there. Come on. We'll go and get them.

R The second picture is correct so there is a tick in box B.

Look at the three pictures for question one now.

Now we are ready to start. Listen carefully. You will hear each recording twice.

R One. Which poster do they decide to buy Terry?

M Terry's got his own room at college now, so why don't we buy him a poster?

F Good idea. He used to like that rock group, you know, the loud one that I don't like.

M Yes I know, but he's got plenty of those. No, what about one of motorcycle racing, because he likes that? Or maybe one of the mountains, as he's living right in the city centre?

F Oh, I think the bikes are a good idea. He'd love that.

R Two. What is the date of the party?

F Are you going to Sophia's 21st birthday party?

M I hope so, but someone told me the date had changed. Is it Saturday 22nd or Sunday 23rd?

F Well, they were going to have it on the 21st, which is actually the date of her birthday, but the band her brother plays in was already booked that night. So they've decided to have it on the Saturday instead.

M Oh, that's good, because I'm off on holiday on Sunday 23rd.

R Three. Which is the missing jacket?

F Hello. Perhaps you can help me. My son left his jacket at the swimming pool yesterday, and I wondered if anyone had found it?

M Yes, I've got three jackets here. Can you describe it to me, please?

F Oh dear, let me think. Umm … it's a child's grey, lightweight jacket. It's the sort which doesn't have a collar, if you know what I mean, but it's got a couple of pockets.

M Ah yes, I think I've got it. When would you like to come and collect it?

R Four. How will they travel to London?

F It's amazing how cheap the plane to London is, and so much faster than the train.

M Yes, I know it's the best way to get there, but have you seen the times? We'd have to get up really early in the morning, and then we'd arrive in London hours before the meeting.

F Yes, but do you really want to drive all that way?

M Well, I don't mind. It's slower than the train, but at least you can choose what time you leave. Let's do that.

F OK.

R Five. Which activity do you have to pay extra for?

F Welcome to the Outdoor Activity Centre. Now, I know your main reason for coming here is to take advantage of our horse-riding facilities, and of course your riding lessons are all included in the price. But don't forget that you also have free use of the swimming pool, and that for a small additional charge you can go for a day's mountain biking in the nearby forest. Now you each begin with an individual riding lesson today, and there's also free extra practice for those who want it this evening.

R Six. What did the boy have for lunch today?

F Do they give you something nice for lunch at the sports centre?

M Yeah, today there was a choice of either fish and chips, soup or a burger.

F Well, that doesn't sound very healthy. I've never known you to eat fish, so I don't suppose you chose that.

M No, I didn't. Then they ran out of burgers before I got to the front of the queue, so I had no choice in the end, but it was alright.

R Seven. Which instrument is the woman going to play?

M Miranda, before you play for us, tell me, why did you choose this particular instrument?

F It's funny, really. My father wanted me to play the piano and I had lessons as a child, but I hated it, and so I never learnt. My sister had a guitar and I was really jealous, because that's what I wanted, but my parents bought me a violin instead. I tried it, but it wasn't the same, and in the end I got my wish, and it was actually my sister who became the violinist.

R That is the end of Part 1.

Page 74 PART 2

R Now turn to Part 2, questions 8–13.

You will hear an interview with a young artist called Mauro Matthews. For each question, put a tick in the correct box.

You now have 45 seconds to look at the questions for Part 2.

Now we are ready to start. Listen carefully. You will hear the recording twice.

F My guest today is a young artist, a painter called Mauro Matthews. Mauro, did you always want to be a painter?

MM Hello. Well I grew up with a love of art, because my mother was always taking me to galleries. But as a child I really wanted to follow my father into the hotel business. But then my older brother trained as a hotel manager and didn't enjoy it. He left to become a cook in the army, and I thought maybe I should do something different, too.

F But you were good at art?

MM Oh, yes. I learnt how to draw at school and did well, in both art and music, which I enjoyed. Although actually my favourite subject was always mathematics — I suppose it has a lot in common with drawing, really. I was good at languages, too, but hopeless in most other subjects.

F So how did your interest in painting develop?

MM By chance, really. My mother's Italian and used to take us to Italy for holidays. One summer, she sent me to a school in Florence to do a course in Italian grammar. I'd learnt to speak it, but made lots of mistakes. The school also did History of Art classes, so I signed up for them, too. It was studying all the wonderful old masters that really made me want to paint.

F So you went to study art at university?

MM That's right. But I didn't enjoy it. You see, most of the classes were about modern art. It wasn't difficult, but it wasn't what I wanted to do. I wanted to paint like the great artists of the past, you know, pictures of people and landscapes, but I wasn't allowed to do that. In the end, I argued with my teachers about it, and although I'd made good friends amongst the other students, I decided to leave.

F Wasn't that a disaster?

MM Not really. I'm still painting. I don't make a living out of it, but I do sell some of my work, and one or two well-known people have asked me to paint them. I've got a job in an art gallery – in the shop, actually – I couldn't pay my bills without that.

F What advice would you give to other young artists?

MM Well, I was lucky because I knew exactly what I wanted to do. A lot of art students just copy each other, because they're frightened to say what they really think. So I'd say, don't listen to the experts or watch what other people are doing, because in the end you have to do the work that's right for you.

R That is the end of Part 2.

Page 74 PART 3

R Now turn to Part 3, questions 14–19.

You will hear a woman giving a talk about holidays in the Caribbean. For each question, fill in the missing information in the numbered space.

You now have 20 seconds to look at Part 3.

Now we are ready to start. Listen carefully. You will hear the recording twice.

F   Hello. I'd like to thank you for coming along this evening to hear about holidays in the Caribbean. I hope that by the end of the evening, you'll have all the information you need to book your holiday.

Now, I'm sure you've all read lots of brochures and guide books, and later I'm going to show you some videos, but first of all let me give you some general information about holidays in the region.

Most holidays from Britain to the Caribbean are all-inclusive, which means that all meals, drinks and watersports are included in the price. This is good, because many of the tourist resorts are a long way away from the towns and cities, and people go there to relax, not to go shopping!

Most of these holidays cost between £650 and £750 per person per week, although this rises to £850 per week in some very well-known resorts, like some of those in Jamaica.

Generally speaking, temperatures tend to average around 27 degrees by day and 15 degrees by night, although rainfall does vary from island to island. The rainy season usually starts in May, and lasts until November in Mexico, but in the Dominican Republic it is finished in August.

Most of the islands in the region have their own currencies, but it is also possible to buy things using US dollars. Take note, however, that euros are not generally accepted, nor are British pounds, so visitors from Europe will need to change their money on arrival.

A valid passport is needed to enter the countries of the Caribbean, but some, such as Cuba, also require you to buy what's called a tourist card, which costs £15 per person. Most airports in the region also have departure taxes, payable as you leave.

So, if there are no questions so far…

R   **That is the end of Part 3.**

Page 75   PART 4

R   **Now turn to Part 4, questions 20–25.**

Look at the six sentences for this part. You will hear a conversation between a girl, Olga, and a boy, Marc. Decide if each sentence is correct or incorrect. If it is correct, put a tick in the box under A for YES. If it is not correct, put a tick in the box under B for NO.

You now have 20 seconds to look at the questions for Part 4.

Now we are ready to start. Listen carefully. You will hear the recording twice.

M   Hi, Olga. I've got the rock concert tickets you asked me to get.

F   Oh, Marc. I'm really grateful, but I'm afraid my mum won't let me go. I hoped to find you before you actually went and bought them. I'm ever so sorry.

M   Look, Olga, you told me you wanted to go, so I bought the tickets. Oh! Why didn't you ask your mum first? You know how difficult she can be.

F   That's not fair, Marc. She's not being difficult, it's just that she's going out that night, so I've got to stay in and look after my little brother.

M   Well, can't somebody else do that? I mean, you could pay one of your mates to do that, rather than waste the £25 for the ticket.

F   What? Oh Marc, I had no idea it would be that expensive! You told me about £15. Where am I going to find that sort of money?

M   Well, all the cheap tickets had gone, and there weren't many left at this price. I didn't want to disappoint you.

F   Well, I can't go, so you'd better ask whether you can get your money back.

M   You can't – it says so on the ticket. Anyway I want to go, and it's no fun on your own.

F   Well ask somebody else, then. I don't mind. If the concert's fully booked, there must be lots of people who'd like to buy that ticket from you.

M   But I wanted to go with *you*.

F   I know, and I'm sorry, but I just can't. Look, why not ask Melanie? I mean, she'd be delighted, because it's her favourite band.

M   Yeah, and I'd have to spend the whole evening with *her*. Think what people would say! No, a better idea is to get Melanie to stay with your brother!

F   I don't think my mum would like that.

M   Well, convince her! Come on, it's worth it!

F   OK, I'll try. But she won't like it.

R   **That is the end of Part 4.**

You now have six minutes to check and copy your answers on to the answer sheet.

You have one more minute.

That is the end of the test.

Notes on the sample Speaking test

Practice Test 1 – Paper 3 Speaking

pages 76–78

On the course cassette/CD, a sample Speaking test has been recorded. It comes between Practice Test 1 and Practice Test 2, which are both Listening tests. In the recording of the Speaking test, actors play the part of students. They perform the test tasks using PET-level language, but without mistakes of grammar, vocabulary or pronunciation.

Students should use the sample Speaking test to help them understand the best way to do the tasks. Remember, the examination tests the ability to speak spontaneously and to interact with another person. This means that it is not possible to learn what to say in advance. It is, however, a good idea to practise and be ready to perform the tasks in the best way.

In the recording, each part of the Speaking test is played separately. The students are using the materials in Practice Test 1 – Speaking on pages 76–8. Students preparing for the PET Speaking test should listen to each part, think about how the students do each task, and then attempt the same tasks themselves. They should not try to remember actual words, as they will need to give their own opinions and ideas. This will, however, be easier for them once they have heard a model.

For each task, a list of things to listen for is included below. Students can either work individually, or in pairs as a classroom activity. Students may need to listen to each part more than once. They should look at the visual materials on pages 77–8 as they listen to Parts 2 and 3.

PART 1

In Part 1, students should answer the examiner's questions. (See page 7 for more information.)

Listen and notice:
- how many questions each student is asked
- how long their answers are
- the types of questions each student is asked
- how the students make what they say interesting

Notice also:
- when the students are asked to spell their names.

PART 2

In Part 2, students talk about the situation in a picture. (See pages 13 and 77 for more information.)

Listen and notice:
- how many times the instructions are given
- how the students begin
- how long each student speaks for
- how each student shows interest in what the other is saying
- how many of the pictures they talk about
- when they reach a decision.

PART 3

In Part 3, each student talks about a photograph. (See pages 40 and 78 for more information.)

Listen and notice:
- the topic of the photographs
- how each student begins
- the type of things they talk about
- what they do if they don't know a word.

PART 4

In Part 4, the students have a discussion on the same topic as Part 3, but giving their own opinions. (See page 43 for more information.)

Listen and notice:
- the two things the students are asked to talk about
- how they begin
- how long each student speaks
- how each student shows interest in what the other is saying
- how they agree and disagree.

Note: the Speaking tests in Ready for PET are sample tests only. They are not actual UCLES past papers.

Tapescript for Practice Test 2

Practice Test 2 – Paper 2 Listening

Page 86   PART 1

RUBRIC = R

R   There are seven questions in this part. For each question there are three pictures and a short recording. Choose the correct picture and put a tick in the box below it.

Before we start, here is an example.

R   Where did the man leave his sunglasses?

M   Oh no! I've lost my sunglasses.
F   Well, you had them on in the car. Perhaps you left them inside?
M   No, I remember taking them off when we parked outside the restaurant. Perhaps I left them in there, or in that shop we went into, just before we had lunch.
F   No, you didn't leave them in the shop, because you put them on the table while we were eating. They must still be there. Come on. We'll go and get them.

R   The second picture is correct so there is a tick in box B.

Look at the three pictures for question one now.

Now we are ready to start. Listen carefully. You will hear each recording twice.

R   One. What time does the film begin?

F   And this evening we have tickets for a film which I think you will find very enjoyable. It's called *Blue Mountain*, and it's a murder mystery set in East Africa. The photography's wonderful. Now, although the film won't actually start until seven forty-five, you need to be at the cinema by seven-thirty at the latest, because they won't keep the reserved seats for us after that time. This means catching the six forty-five bus from outside the school gates. OK?

R   Two. What does the man want to borrow?

M   Hello, sorry to trouble you, but I've come to tie up Mrs. Carter's rose bushes that were blown down in the storm. I've brought some string with me, but I have forgotten my penknife. So I was wondering if you had a pair of scissors that I could borrow to cut the string with?
F   Yes, of course. Just a minute, I'll get them for you.

R   Three. What has the girl forgotten?

F   I can't understand it. I laid everything out on my bed: toothbrush, toothpaste, shampoo, soap dish – I checked it was all there, and then put it in my bag. But when I got to my hotel room, the toothpaste had somehow disappeared. It's so annoying, because you get free soap and shampoo in this hotel anyway – so I've forgotten the one thing I need!

R   Four. Which hat will Yasmin wear in the play?

M   I hear you've been making hats for the school play.
F   That's right. Yasmin's teacher asked if anyone's mum knew how to make hats, and she said I did. Well, I did make her a baseball cap once, but I'm not an expert! Anyway, for the play, they wanted a big straw one with lots of flowers on for Yasmin's friend Amy, who's playing a princess – and a crown for Yasmin herself, because she's going to be the queen. And you know, I really enjoyed it!

R   Five. What has the team captain just broken?

M   And there are more problems for Foxton United Football Club, I'm afraid. Last week, one of their top players fell and broke his ankle during the match against Brent Rovers, and now the team captain, Billy Knight, has broken an arm in an accident at home. Billy slipped on a piece of loose carpet and fell down the stairs. This is very bad news for Billy, who injured his foot last year and has only been playing again for a few weeks.

R   Six. Where will they have the picnic?

M   I'm getting hungry. Can't we stop walking now and have our picnic? We could sit under that tree over there.

F Oh, it's beginning to get cold. Let's sit in the sun. How about over there next to the river, or on those rocks over there?

M Well I'm hot as well as hungry, so I'd prefer to sit in the shade. Anyway if we sit by the river, insects will bite us!

F OK. I don't mind really. We'll sit where you want.

R **Seven. Which bus goes to the airport?**

F Excuse me. Will the number 24 bus take me to the airport?

M Well, it does go in that direction, but it doesn't actually go as far as the airport, so you'd have a bit of a walk! Umm … the bus you need is the number 27, but it doesn't go from here, I'm afraid. You need to get the number 26 to the railway station and then change. You can catch the airport bus from there.

F Oh, that's no good, I'm in a hurry!

R **That is the end of Part 1.**

Page 87   PART 2

R **Now turn to Part 2, questions 8–13.**

You will hear part of a radio programme about a holiday in Italy where you learn how to cook. For each question, put a tick in the correct box.

You now have 45 seconds to look at the questions for Part 2.

Now we are ready to start. Listen carefully. You will hear the recording twice.

F Next in the programme, Adrian Layton tells us about his unusual holiday in Italy.

AL I love Italian food and I've always wanted to learn how to make it properly. There are lots of courses you can do in England, you see advertisements in the newspapers, but I've never really had time to go on one. Then a friend told me about a cooking course in Italy where a famous chef was the teacher. I'd seen her on television, so I knew it would be good, and I decided to go.

The course took place in a beautiful eighteenth-century house on an island in the south of Italy. As I expected, the weather was lovely, even in September, but I was surprised that there weren't many tourists there, because the local beaches are just as good as the guidebooks say.

There are also some Ancient Greek and Roman ruins to visit – although, like most ruins, there isn't really much to see.

Each day, we woke up early and had breakfast together. Lessons started soon afterwards. The teacher was *excellent*. She has worked in lots of famous restaurants and I really felt that I was learning a professional skill – it wasn't like being at school at all. Of course, the best bit was eating the things we'd prepared for lunch!

We made some *very* tasty dishes. I learnt to make fresh pasta, which I'd always wanted to do, but my favourite lesson was the one where we learnt to make a pizza, which was then cooked in a special oven. The one I made was rather a strange shape, but it tasted good and I still felt very proud of it.

It was a small group, which was good for the lessons, but the other people were all older than me, mostly couples in their thirties and forties. I was on my own and I had hoped to make new friends of my own age. So that was a bit disappointing. But the people were very nice, and I was never lonely because we did everything together.

At the end of the week, we received a pack with all the recipes we'd made. I've cooked most of them for my friends since I've been home – they can't *believe* what a good cook I am! Two of them have booked the same course next year as a result. But I'm trying something different. There's a similar course in Thailand, learning how to make green curry and spicy fishcakes. It should be great!

R **That is the end of Part 2.**

Page 87   PART 3

R **Now turn to Part 3, questions 14–19.**

You will hear a radio announcement about a film club. For each question, fill in the missing information in the numbered space.

You now have 20 seconds to look at Part 3.

Now we are ready to start. Listen carefully. You will hear the recording twice.

F … And now we have news about The Valley Film Club. If you would like to join The Film Club, or if you are already a member and you would like to continue for another year, it's time to pay your annual membership fee. This will cost you £47.50. That's a slight increase on last year's fee of £46.00, but there's still a 20% discount for students.

So what do you get for your money? The Film Club meets three times a week, on Tuesday, Thursday and Saturday evenings. On Tuesdays, you can see European films. These are in the original language with subtitles. On Thursdays, you can see action movies, and on Saturdays there is always a romantic comedy. Members can see these films for free, although guests have to pay.

Then, each year, The Film Club organizes a week-long film festival. This is usually held in late April or May, but this year it will be later than usual, being held in the first week of June. Club members get the chance to choose some of the films which are shown, and this year there is a special theme. All of the films will be on the topic of wildlife. It should be very interesting.

Then, The Film Club also organizes various special events throughout the year. In November, for example, a week of horror films replaces the normal programme, with some famous films and also some less well-known examples for you to go and see – if you're brave enough!

Then, in August, there's a week of cartoons. These come from all over the world and are not all for children. There'll be some old favourites, however, so that's certainly something for all the family to look forward to.

If you'd like more information…

R   That is the end of Part 3.

Page 88   PART 4

R   Now turn to Part 4, questions 20–25.

Look at the six sentences for this part. You will hear a conversation between a girl, Lucy, and a boy, Tony. Decide if each sentence is correct or incorrect. If it is correct, put a tick in the box under A for YES. If it is not correct, put a tick in the box under B for NO.

You now have 20 seconds to look at the questions for Part 4.

Now we are ready to start. Listen carefully. You will hear the recording twice.

M   Lucy!

F   Hi Tony! I heard that you've just got a new motorbike. Is that true?

M   Well, I haven't actually got it yet, but I'm getting one soon. Anyway, how did you know? It's meant to be a secret.

F   Oh, you know, I hear most things in this town. But what I don't understand is where the money's coming from. I thought you were saving to go to Canada next summer?

M   Oh, I am. I've got enough for the ticket. All I need now is spending money, because I'll be staying with some cousins once I'm over there.

F   Lucky you. So come on, how can you afford a motorbike, as well as that?

M   Well, if you must know, my uncle's giving me the bike as a twenty-first birthday present. It belongs to my cousin. He's had it for two years, but he hasn't used it very much because it's too big for him, really, so now he's buying a car instead.

F   Your family sounds really great – free holidays, expensive gifts. It's not fair, I never get anything out of mine!

M   Oh, yeah. And who paid for you to go on that skiing holiday last year?

F   That was different. I saved up half of the money and my dad paid the rest. That was the agreement. *You* seem to get everything for nothing. Anyway, when can we expect to see this bike?

M   On Wednesday.

F   Are you going to take me out for a ride on it?

M   I don't know, Lucy. I think I need to get used to it myself before I start taking passengers. It's quite a large bike, you know.

F   Oh, don't worry about that. I'm used to handling big bikes. If you're nervous, I'll sit in front and you can be the passenger.

M   Look, I'm not sure, Lucy. Let's wait and see. I'm not making any promises.

F   Oh, Tony. You are boring sometimes!

R   That is the end of Part 4.

You now have six minutes to check and copy your answers onto the answer sheet.

You have one more minute.

That is the end of the test.

Examples of student writing

In PET Writing Part 2, students are required to write a short communicative message, and in PET Writing Part 3 they have to write either an informal letter or a story. (For more details refer to pages 10, 37 and 38.)

A maximum of 5 marks are available in PET Writing Part 2. In this part, the focus of assessment is on successful communication of the message. Students will score high marks if they have conveyed the three points in the instructions clearly.

In PET Writing Part 3, 15 marks are available. The focus of assessment in this part is the student's ability to organize ideas clearly and to convey them using a range of language. Assessment is based on the correct use of spelling and punctuation; on accurate and appropriate use of a variety of grammatical structures; and on the use of topic-related vocabulary and linking words.

At this level, students are not expected to produce writing which is completely free from errors. A mistake that does not prevent the writer from being understood is considered less serious than a mistake that interferes with communication. Students are given credit for being ambitious in attempting a range of different structures, even if they make some errors.

The following examples were written by students attempting the Practice Tests on pages 71–72 and 84–85. The examiner's comment 'adequate attempt' indicates the minimum standard of writing necessary to achieve a pass at PET level.

Practice Test 1, Writing Part 2

1

> Dear Chris,
> Thank you very much to invite me to have dinner with you and your cousins in your house. I really enjoyed playing with them the guitar. This weekend I'm going with some friends to the cinema. Would you like to come?
> Love,
> Laura

Examiner's comment: 5 marks
The three points in the instructions for this task are included and expressed clearly. The minor language errors ('to invite', 'with them the guitar') don't prevent the message from being understood.

2

> Dear Chris
> Thank you for give me an unforgettable evening. I really enjoyed the food and the music. Did anybody told you that you are a good singer and a good chef. If you don't mind, I'd glad to have the recipe. I can make it for myself.
> Bye,
> Tang

Examiner's comment: 3 marks
One of the points from the instructions for this task ('invite Chris to do something with you') has been left out, so this student can't score more than 3 marks. However, the other two points are expressed clearly in spite of some language errors ('for give', 'Did anybody told', 'I'd glad').

Practice Test 1, Writing Part 3 (letter)

3

> Dear Friend,
> Thank you for your letter. I didn't know you played the guitar and sang in a rock band! When did you start it? I would like to listen to your music because I like rock music too! In fact, I enjoy listen to all kinds of music, above all when I study because it relaxes myself.
> Although I'm music's great fan, I'm sorry to say I can't play a musical instrument. When I was a child, I learned piano for a few years. But now I already forgot everything. If I continued learning play the piano, I would play very well now!
> I'm looking forward to hear your music someday. Please write to me again soon.
> Your friend,
> Dario

Examiner's comment: very good attempt
This student writes confidently and is ambitious in his use of language. He uses a mixture of past and present tenses appropriately, and attempts some complex sentence patterns with 'when', 'because', 'although' and 'if'. He demonstrates good control of music-related vocabulary ('played the guitar', 'sang in a rock band', 'listen to your music', 'all kinds of music', 'play a musical instrument', 'learned piano'), although much of this is supplied by the input text. Ideas are clearly organized in paragraphs and some simple linking devices are used: 'too', 'in fact', 'above all', 'but'. The letter begins and ends in an appropriate way. There are a few minor errors ('enjoy listen', 'relaxes myself' etc), but they do not prevent communication of the ideas.

4

> Dear Penfriend,
> Thank you I received your letter on Monday 12th.
> It's good for me know about the kind of music you like.
>   When you come to visit me I'll take you to hear some rock music. I hope you'll like it because this group it's famous in my country. I went to see them sometime ago I like them very much. I can play the guitar but not very well and I don't like to sing. I sometimes play the guitar with my brother he's very good at play the guitar and he's teaching me how to play the guitar.
>   I hope you are well write to me soon.
> Yours sincerely
> Vidal

Examiner's comment: adequate attempt

This student's use of language is not very ambitious and lacks variety. However, he uses present, past and future tenses appropriately and attempts sentence patterns with *'when'* and *'because'*. There is use of music-related vocabulary, but it relies heavily on language from the input text and there is unnecessary repetition of *'play the guitar'*. The ideas are organized in paragraphs and there is use of the linking words *'and'* and *'but'*. Lack of appropriate punctuation, however, means that sentences sometimes run together (*'I went to see them sometime ago I like them very much'*, *'I hope you are well write to me soon'*). The letter begins and ends in a suitable way, although the very first sentence is not quite appropriate for an informal letter. There are some errors (*'good for me know'*, *'this group it's'*, *'good at play'*), but they do not impede communication.

5

> I like listening the guitar sound. The rock musique, it's not my favourite but something I enjoyed to listen it.
>   Now, I'm in the school of sing, I fancy it, my voice is not bad precisely I would like to play a musical instrument like you, "the guitar".
>   I will write to you my first sing.

Examiner's comment: poor attempt

It is difficult to make an assessment of this student's work, as it is so short. There is evidence of some control of verb forms (*'I like listening'*, *'I will write'*), and there is some use of appropriate vocabulary (*'sound'*, *'favourite'*, *'voice'*) but other words are misused (*'sing'*, *'fancy'*, *'precisely'*). Erratic punctuation adds to the incoherence. Although the piece mentions *'you'*, the writer makes no attempt to follow letter-writing conventions by addressing the friend directly, introducing or finishing off the letter, or signing it.

Practice Test 1, Writing Part 3 (story)

6

> The New Shoes
> It was winter, the coldest one in years. Alma was alone waiting for her familly. She was an old lady, very pretty in her youth but now her face looks tired and sad. Her husband had died during the war when she was pregnanted. After that she didn't meet another man because she was still fall in love with her husband died. She was sitting in her old armchair when the bell rang. It was the postman with a box and a letter which said We are so sorry but We couldn't going to visit you this year.
>   She opened the box and she saw a pretty pair of new shoes. She put them in the bin because she wanted her familly, no any silly shoes.

Examiner's comment: very good attempt

This student uses language ambitiously to tell an interesting story. She has good control of past tenses, although there is one slip (*'looks'*). She makes a good attempt to use complex sentence patterns with *'when'*, *'which'* and *'because'*. There is a good range of vocabulary to tell the story, most of it used effectively (*'It was winter, the coldest one in years'*, *'alone waiting'*, *'very pretty in her youth'*), although some of it is awkward (*'she was still fall in love with her husband died'*). There are a couple of spelling mistakes (*'familly'*, *'pregnanted'*). A good attempt is made to organize the narrative into paragraphs and make use of linking devices (*'but'*, *'after that'*), and the story reaches a clear resolution. There are some errors (*'couldn't going'*, *'no'*), but they don't impede communication.

7

> The New shoes
> One day, I went to Camden Town to buy some shoes. Here you can find all things that you want. It's strange place. I found a small shop under some stairs. The shop assistant was a small chinese woman. I saw a very pretty shoes, the woman gave and I try it. I fell in love with a shoes and I bought it.
>   When I arrived my home I put it and I went to the kichen to show it to my mother. She listened to me but she couldn't saw me. This shoes were a magic shoes. If I put nobody saw me. It was fantastic. But I get up and my dream finished.

Examiner's comment: adequate attempt

The language in this story is unambitious, but adequate. The student's control of past tenses is generally sound, with some lapses (*'couldn't saw'*, *'get up'*). An attempt is made to use some complex sentence patterns with *'that'*, *'when'* and *'If'*. There are several errors, the most serious being the failure to use plural agreement between *'shoes'*, and determiners and pronouns. The range of vocabulary is just adequate to tell the story, although there is some misuse of lexical items (*'try'* for *'try on'*, *'put'* for *'put on'*, *'listened'* for *'heard'*, and *'get up'* for *'woke up'*). These errors generally do not impede communication, although they require the reader to make some effort. There is an attempt to organize ideas into paragraphs. The narrative starts well with a clear setting of the scene, and the story is resolved satisfactorily.

8

> The New Shoes
> I always cost many times to look for fit
> shoes in my legs.
> My favorite shoes are not only beautiful but
> also comfortable.
> As I am a short woman, so I used to wear
> high heels.
> But the other day, I found brown deck shoes
> at near shop.
> It was very nice, so I tried it on.
> It was perfect fit for me, so I bought it.
> Nex time, when I go to somewhere, I would
> like to wear the new shoes.

Examiner's comment: inadequate attempt

This student's language is rather limited, although an attempt is made to tell the story. Past tenses are used appropriately, but *'I used to'* is misused. Some effort is made to employ a complex sentence pattern, but this is either repetitive (*'It was ..., so I ...'*) or incorrect (*'As I am a short woman, so I ...'*). There is some appropriate vocabulary (*'comfortable'*, *'high heels'*, *'deck shoes'*, *'tried it on'*, *'perfect fit'*), but understanding some phrasing demands considerable effort from the reader (*'I always cost many times to look for fit shoes in my legs'*). Misuse of the pronoun *'it'*, instead of *'they/them'*, also impedes communication. Some time phrases and other linking devices (*'But the other day'*, *'Nex time'*) are used, but the narrative is mostly written at sentence level, with each sentence beginning on a new line. No attempt is made to organize ideas into paragraphs. The student is also penalized because the story is rather short.

Practice Test 2, Writing Part 2

9

> To: Robin
> From: Marina
>
> I have started my English course one
> month ago. It's a bit of hard. Sometimes
> it's boring to memorize many new words.
> But the teacher's very kind and humorous.
> I like her. Tell me something about you.
> Marina

Examiner's comment: 5 marks

The three points in the instructions for this task are included and expressed clearly. The minor language errors (*'I have started'*, *'a bit of hard'*) don't prevent the message from being communicated.

10

> Hello!
> I am very happy, because I am studying paint
> at the Art College. I enjoy myself. My class is
> very interesting. I am studying every day at 8
> am – 10 am and I improved my oil picture.
> Your, Olga

Examiner's comment: 3 marks

One of the points from the instructions for this task (*'describe the teacher'*) has been left out, so the student can't score more than 3 marks. However, the other two points are expressed reasonably clearly, in spite of some language errors (*'paint'*, *'at 8 am - 10 am'*, *'I improved my oil picture'*).

Practice Test 2, Writing Part 3 (letter)

11

> Hello friends.
> Congratulation!
> How is your new house, new days, new life? I'm so
> sorry I couldn't be your wedding, but I could know
> what a wonderful party it was from your photos.
>   A typical Japanese wedding has two events.
> They are a marriage celemony and wedding
> reception. A celemony is held with bride & groom,
> relative, a few close friend at church or shrine.
> After celemony finished, big reception is held at a
> high-class hotel. Bride and groom enter the hall with
> music. The important people give a speech. And,
> they exchange the wedding rings again, cut the
> wedding cake.
>   While attendace are eating and chatting, a
> bride cahage her costume two or three times. Is it
> funny thing, isn't it?
> Your friend, Tomoko

Examiner's comment: good attempt

This student uses language fairly ambitiously. There is good control of verb forms and although there are some errors, they do not impede communication (*'Is it funny thing, isn't it?'*). The sentence structure is mostly simple, but some complex patterns are attempted with *'after'* and *'while'*. There is a very wide range of appropriate vocabulary, but there are also a couple of bad spelling errors where the meaning has to be guessed at (*'attendace'*, *'cahage'*). There is an attempt to organize ideas into paragraphs, but linking of ideas is limited to *'but'* and *'and'*. The letter has a very good introductory paragraph, but ends rather abruptly.

12

> Dear Charles and Nancy,
> How are you? I'm fine and I'm very sorry I couldn't come to your wedding. I've already seen your photos and they are very nice and interested.
> When I was seeing your photos I remember my brother's wedding 2 mouths ago, which was a tipical celebration in my country. My brother sad in front of evrybody 'I'll take you Katia for all my life' and after that evryone though 'who is Katia?' because the bride was Alicia. I think maybe never in her life the bride forgive my brother.
> See you soon, take care
> Eloy

Examiner's comment: adequate attempt

The language control in this letter is rather erratic, but in spite of the errors ('couldn't came', 'interested', 'mouths', 'sad', 'evrybody', 'forgive', etc) the message is communicated. There is an attempt to use some complex sentence patterns with 'when', 'which' and 'because'. The range of vocabulary is adequate ('remember', 'tipical celebration', 'bride', 'forgive'). The ideas are organized into paragraphs, and use is made of the linking phrase 'after that'. The letter begins and ends appropriately.

Practice Test 2, Writing Part 3 (story)

13

> Harry often went to the beach although he couldn't swim. He didn't like water because when he was a baby he had fallen into a washing machine. Still he dreams nightmares with that terrible machine.
> One day he met a nice girl in the beach. They were chatting all the day and he fell in great love. One warm night they were sitting down on the sea wall. Suddenly Harry wanted to kiss his friend but it was the first time and she was so surprised that she moved falling in the deep water. She couldn't get out and nobody was nearby that place who could help her. Harry was very frightened but in the end he jumped in the sea and he saved his friend's life.
> Now they are married and Harry likes swimming in the sea.

Examiner's comment: very good attempt

This student tells the story confidently and uses some ambitious language. She shows consistent control of past tenses ('had fallen', 'met', 'were sitting', etc) and attempts some complex sentence patterns using 'because', 'so surprised ... that', 'who'. She uses a range of appropriate vocabulary to tell the story ('washing machine', 'nightmares', 'chatting', 'fell in love', 'sea wall', 'kiss', 'surprised', 'deep', 'frightened', 'saved ... life', 'married'). The ideas are organized clearly in paragraphs, with some appropriate linking words and expressions of time to move the story along ('Still', 'One day', 'One warm night', 'Suddenly', 'but', 'in the end', 'Now'). The story is resolved neatly. There are very few errors.

14

> Harry often went to the beach although he couldn't swim. He decided to sunbathe and sleep as well. Also the beach had very crowd. Then he went at the hotel and met with him friends. They went to the restaurant and they had the lunch.
> As soon as they finiched, they went to the shoopin in the central city. They bought a few souvenirs. On the other hand it's a very expensive city.
> When they finiched the shooping, they had a look round the city. They saw monuments, castles, cathedrals, fountains, museums, statues, etc.
> After they went to the disco and other day they came back they house.
> Finality they had wonderful holiday.

Examiner's comment: adequate attempt

This is an unambitious story and the language is a bit erratic. There is good control of past tenses and some attempt to use complex sentence patterns with 'As soon as' and 'when'. Although they do not generally impede communication, there are many errors and spelling mistakes ('had very crowd', 'at the hotel', 'met with him friends', 'had the lunch', 'finiched', 'shoopin', 'they house', 'Finality'). There is a good range of vocabulary ('decided', 'sunbathe', 'souvenirs', 'expensive', 'had a look round', 'monuments, castles, cathedrals, fountains, museums, statues') and the student attempts to use linking devices ('as well', 'Then'), but they are not always used correctly. The student makes an attempt to organize ideas into paragraphs and to bring the story to a resolution, but the strategy of telling the story as a list of events is not very effective.

Wordlist

Unit 1 Lesson 1
advice
block capitals
to collect
to complete (a form)
computer games
(to go) dancing
date of birth
details
driving
to enjoy
to explain
free time
hill walking
(to go) horse riding
instruction
to be interested (in s.thing)
interesting
Internet
keep-fit exercises
notice
occupation
package
personal
to play
shop assistant
to sign (your name)
signature
to spell
to study
suggestion
to surf (the Internet)
surname
warning
watersports
windsurfing

Unit 1 Lesson 2
to accept
to agree
armchair
to attend
books
to brush
to check
climate
to comb
daily
to describe
desk
to dial
dishes
to dust
to feed
to forget
furniture
(a pair of) glasses
hair
to hand in
to imagine
international
interview
to invent
invention
to iron
to join in
make-up
medicine
meeting
message
mirror
to miss
mobile phone
to offer
palace
parcel
pet
philosopher
(what a) pity
to plug in
popular
to put away
to put on
to put up
radio
scientist
shirt

shoelaces
(a pair of) shoes
situation
soap
(a pair of) socks
to suggest
to take off
teeth
to thank
to tidy
to tie
to turn on
to turn up
umbrella
walkman
(to do the) washing-up
worried

Unit 2 Lesson 1
blackboard
boring
cakes
CD (compact disc)
to cook
correct
the cost (of s.thing)
document
(to send an) e-mail
enjoyable
equipment
favourite
to fry (an egg)
fun
to be good (at s.thing)
hobby
incorrect
ingredients
keyboard
to last
length
to look forward (to s.thing)
magazines
mouse
newspaper
to respond
screen
stuff
textbook
useful
video cassette
video player
videotape

Unit 2 Lesson 2
adult
adventure story
to advertise
amusing
autobiography
to belong (to s.body)
biography
bookshop
to borrow
to take care
charming
to create
cruel
damage
danger
daughter
deadly
delighted
design
dinosaur
to disappear
to discover
distant
to encourage
enemy
excitement
exciting
film star
gossip
grandson
to guide

to happen
heavy
hero
horror
humour
to hunt (for s.thing)
(a police) inspector
to investigate
to invite
journey
kind
to lend
to look for
to manage (to do s.thing)
marvellous
murder
mystery
old-fashioned
opinion
to pass (time)
planet
powerful
to prepare
to prove
to publish
realistic
to recognize
to request
to respect
romance
science fiction
secret
shadow
to shoot
spaceship
space travel
a spoonful (of s.thing)
stage
to steal
stormy
strange
successful
suitable
surprise
teenager
thriller
universe
victim
visitor
to win
wise

Unit 3 Lesson 1
accommodation
answerphone
arrangements
available
belongings
binoculars
booking
brochure
(to go) camping
campsite
credit card
destination
to discuss
downstairs
employee
excursion
experience
expert
facilities
first-aid kit
guest house
guidebook
handicrafts
hotel
luggage
map
market
minimum
mosquito net
nervous
nightlife
official
to pack

package holiday
passenger
photographs
(to have a) picnic
postcards
preparation
to prevent
to provide (s.thing for s.body)
to put up
(to make a) reservation
to run out (of s.thing)
scenery
shells
shower
sightseeing
souvenirs
(to go) sunbathing
(a pair of) sunglasses
suntan lotion
to supply
to take turns
tinned food
tour
training course
travel agency
trip
truck
unattended
value
variety
vegetables
vehicle
wallet
wildlife

Unit 3 Lesson 2
to accompany
advertisement
appearance
application form
to apply (for a job)
architect
artist
bank clerk
biologist
businessman/woman
chemist
choice
to decide
decision
doctor
to earn (a salary)
to employ
employment
engineer
to fill in (a form)
fortunately
to get up
to govern
government
hard work
insurance
journalist
lawyer
lift
lucky
manager
microscope
musician
to organize
physicist
to pick (s.one) up
police officer
profession
qualification
recording studio
responsible
to retire
retirement
rules
satisfactory
staff
stressful
strike
to succeed
success
traffic

typical
unfamiliar
uniform
unsuitable
unusual
vegetarian

Unit 4 Lesson 1
balcony
basement
bath
bathroom
bedroom
bedside table
blanket
blinds
block of flats
calculator
chest of drawers
coffee table
cooker
curtains
cushions
dining room
dishwasher
dressing table
fridge
garage
garden
hairdryer
hallway
kitchen
lamp
living room
mirror
packed lunch
pillows
to remember
seaside
shampoo
sheet
sink
sofa
stairs
storeroom
towel (rail)
vase
wardrobe
washbasin
waterproof
wood

Unit 4 Lesson 2
to advise
amount
amusing
anxious
attitude
attractive
blond(e)
bored
boring
careful
careless
celebration
cheerful
to compare
to complain
confident
to correspond
curly
to develop
development
dull
education
fair
foolish
funny
hard-working
high school
honest
intelligence
lazy
to measure
middle-aged
miserable
to point
pretty

professor
psychologist
to recommend
serious
shy
slim
smart
to smile
speed
strong
tired
truthful
ugly
understanding
university
weak

Unit 5 Lesson 1
admission
to arrange
attraction
breakage
ceiling
changing rooms
to climb
collection
department store
discount
display
entrance (fee)
to exhibit
giftshop
to hire
home-made
in advance
to inform
items
leaflet
picture gallery
pleasant
plenty
public
reasonable
to receive
refreshments
representative
to reserve
ruin
sports centre
surrounding
to touch
traditional
view
weigh
well-known

Unit 5 Lesson 2
appointment
arrival
attendant
bank account
boarding pass
carriage
to catch
to check in
to check out (of)
convenient
to cross out
to disturb
to draw out
driver
explanation
fare
to fill in (a form)
forename
furnished
gate
to get in
to get off
to get on
to give in
to hurry up
instead of
to land
to lend
license
luggage
meter

passenger
personal
pilot
platform
position
report
station
stop
to switch on
to take off
ticket
timetable
to turn over
underground

Unit 6 Lesson 1
acceptance
bargain
belt
boot
buttons
charge
cheque
clothing
collar
cotton
department
electrical
escalator
example
fashion
fashionable
goods
invitation
lift
out of order
paragraph
pocket
reason
receipt
receive
reduce
refusal
repair
sale
shopping centre
silk
skirt
sleeve
speciality
to spend
spices
spots
stall
street market
stripes
sweater
tie
(a pair of) tights
tip
to try on
topic
upstairs
vegetables
wool
zip

Unit 6 Lesson 2
advantage
convenient
crowded
dangerous
dirty
employment
entertainment
forest
fresh air
inconvenient
lonely
noisy
objects
peaceful
polluted
relaxing

rice
safe
spoon
stressful
sunny
traffic
transport
vehicle
way (of life)

Unit 7 Lesson 1
to add
bananas
beans
beef
burgers
butter
carrots
cheese
chicken
duck
fork
garlic
grapes
hard-boiled egg
herbs
impressive
knife
lamb
mayonnaise
to mix (together)
mixing bowl
mixture
mushrooms
olives
onions
oranges
owl
peas
pepper
plums
potato
to pour
recipe
salt
sausages
seeds
selection
sharp
snack
a spoonful (of
    s.thing)
steak
tasty
tomatoes
tomato sauce
triangle
tuna fish

Unit 7 Lesson 2
to afford
to allow
to annoy
argument
average
to blame
circumstances
cupboard
divide
dizzy
early
to expect
fancy
to find
to fit
fussy
knock
to lead to
likely
lucky
to mind
miserable
to operate
opinion

privacy
regret
relationship
to repair
to review
selfish
to separate
to share
shelf
storage
tidiness
to tidy up
wardrobe

Unit 8 Lesson 1
to appear
to attack
bat
to be born
bear
bee
to breathe
brilliant
to bury
changeable
cheerful
chicken
clear
clouds
coal
coast
cool
countryside
cow
damp
to defend
depressed
to destroy
to dig up
disease
dolphin
to dry up
dull
dusty
elephant
encouraging
environment
extraordinary
extremely
eyesight
to fall down
fields
to fight
fine
to fly
foggy
forecast
freezing
frost
giraffe
gold
goldfish
gorilla
height
horse
human
hunger
inhabitants
iron
jump
kick
kitten
lightning
minerals
mist
monkey
mouse
nature
to overtake
owner
pavement
pet
to pick
pigeon

to pollute
to pour
poverty
to prevent
rabbit
rain
to reach
to realize
to rescue
rubbish
to set out
shark
shower
to slip
snake
snow
spider
to spoil
storms
to strike
to suffer
sunshine
to tear
thunder
tiger
tongue
urgent
warm
to watch
weather
to weigh
wind

Unit 8 Lesson 2
to admire
beach
border
to break (down)
bush
camel
canal
canoe
cave
cliff
climb
continent
to cross
desert
director
distance
district
eagle
edge
to float
to flood
foreign
frontier
to hang
hole
interval
irrigation
island
jungle
local
location
mountain
mud
nest
on foot
on horseback
passport
path
project
to promise
to provide
restful
rock
row
ruins
sand
scenery
to set (the video)
shade
to shine

shore
to smell
soil
speed
stream
temperature
to tour
track
villain
waterfall
wave
website

Unit 9 Lesson 1
adventurer
to attend
balloon
baseball
to brush
circus
clown
crab
to discover
driving test
entertainment
envelope
facts
to fail
to feed
flower
frightened
golf
ground
gymnastics
hammer
handle
hockey
to introduce
to invent
judo
juggling
nails
needle
net
notepaper
paint
pins
poetry
pot
to present
racket
refreshing
safety (rules)
sailing
scissors
seeds
skiing
skill
to slide
spade
stamp
table tennis
to take up
training
tunnel
watering can
windsurfing
workshop

Unit 9 Lesson 2
accident
to ache
ambulance
aspirin
benefit
blood
to consider
to cure
deaf
deep
dentist
disease
documentary
to fall over

flu
Get well!
grateful
healthy
hearing (aid)
hospital
hurt
jogging
lifestyle
to look (after)
opportunity
patient
sickness
sore throat
stress
to take care (of)
toothache
unhealthy
valuable

Unit 10 Lesson 1
action (film)
actor
audience
backing (group)
camera
channel
characters
chat room
to clap
clubbing
to come up
comedian
commercial
crew
curtain
dancer
delicious
director
disc jockey
drummer
film critic
interval
interviewer
lead (singer)
lines
performance
pianist
play
plot
pop group
to practise
presenter
programme
region
reviews
screen
series
singer
soap opera
(to be) sold out
stage
studio
violinist
wet

Unit 10 Lesson 2
communication
confused
to contact
face-to-face
fax
letters
misunderstanding
to pay attention
to phone
recent
relaxed
respect (for)
screen
skills
word-processing